A PRIMER

OF

CHESS

BY

José R. Capablanca

A HARVEST BOOK
HARCOURT BRACE & COMPANY
San Diego   New York   London

Requests for permission to make copies
of any part of the work should be mailed to:
Permissions Department, Harcourt Brace & Company,
6277 Sea Harbor Drive, Orlando, Florida 32887-6777.

Library of Congress Cataloging-in-Publication Data
Capablanca, José Raúl, 1888–1942.
A primer of chess.
(A Harvest book) .
Reprint. Originally published: New York:
Harcourt, Brace, Jovanovich, 1977, c1963.
1. Chess. I. Title.
GV1446.C29   1983   794.1   83-8470
ISBN 0-15-673900-3

Printed in the United States of America
H J K I G

Author's Note

The author wishes to acknowledge his obligation to Professor Ernest Hunter Wright for his most valuable assistance in preparing the manuscripts for publication and to Dr. B. M. Anderson, Jr., for his preface.

Ernest Hunter Wright, professor of English at Columbia University for the last twenty-five years, is a very good and enthusiastic chess player. He is the author of a book entitled *The Meaning of Rousseau* and is the editor-in-chief of *Richards Cyclopedia* for juveniles.

B. M. Anderson, Jr., Ph.D., is one of the world's leading economists. He was professor of economics both at Harvard and Columbia Universities, and he is today economic adviser to one of the largest banks in New York City. His technical training included not only practical money and banking, but also philosophy, sociology, and economic theory. With it all he is a first-class chess player.

Contents

PART I

PART III

Part One

Introduction

THE object of this book is to fill an existing need in chess literature. Thirteen years ago I wrote a treatise called " Chess Fundamentals " bringing out a number of things which had never appeared in a chess book. " Chess Fundamentals " as the title explains covers all the principles in chess, but it does not deal so minutely as this book will with the things that beginners need to know. When " Chess Fundamentals " appeared, I had intended to write two other treatises related to each other and to " Chess Fundamentals," thus making a complete unit. " A Primer of Chess " is one of these two treatises. A little later the third book will appear and naturally it will deal only with that part of the game which has been least discussed in the first two. The third volume will treat mainly of the openings. The middle game and the end game will be mentioned only in so far as they are related to the openings treated in the text. All of this is said with the intention of impressing upon the reader the close relation that will exist between a " Primer of Chess " and " Chess Fundamentals." Although every effort will be made in the present book to refer as little as possible to " Chess Fundamentals," the reader will realize that some reference to " Chess Fundamentals " will be necessary from time to time.

In writing for beginners I shall strive to make the

language simple and concise in the aim of making it as easy as possible for any one to learn to play without the aid of a teacher.

A SHORT SKETCH OF THE HISTORY OF CHESS

Many colourful tales have been told about the origin and history of chess. The truth about the origin is really unknown. We can trace the story of the game back to 3000 B.C. and then we lose the thread as with so many other things in history. Chess has not always been played just as it is today. In Europe the last change took place some hundred years ago. Until recently the game has been played under different rules in different countries and among different races, oriental and occidental. Years ago, while playing a friendly game with the Emir of Transjordania, I found that he was used to castling in a different way from ours; and a short time ago I was informed by Mir Sultan Khan, the leading player of Great Britain, that in his native country of India he had originally learned to play the game under quite different rules: castling was totally different and Pawns never moved more than one square at a time, while in our game they are permitted to move two squares on the first move. No doubt in other places other differences have existed, but in all lands the European influence has now prevailed and at last the game can be said to be a universal pastime under the same rules everywhere.

There is no doubt that our game as played today is Medieval in its character. It is a warlike and courtly game, as may be seen from the names and action of the pieces. It was the game of kings and it is today the king of games. The Pawns may be said to represent the yeomen of the guards, covering and battling in front of the Knights, Bishops and Royal Personages. The Knights, Bishops, King and Queen are self-explanatory, while the Rooks or Castles represent the strongholds of the Noblemen. If all these titled personages have disappeared from many countries of the world, the game of chess has remained a game of social distinction which taxes the highest effort of the human mind.

For a long time it was felt that chess was a pastime for the privileged classes only, but now the game is advocated by educators and philosophers as excellent training for any mind. Truly enough it is difficult to play chess well, but quite as truly it is easy to learn the elements of the game; and when once these have been learned, the practice of them will provide more enjoyment and satisfaction than will come from any other game known to man.

Chapter I

THE GAME, THE MEN, THEIR MOVES, OBJECT OF THE GAME

To those who are uninitiated in its mysteries the game of chess seems much too complicated for the average individual. But this is really not the case. With a little application the average person should be able to play the game after ten or twelve lessons.

I. THE GAME

The game of chess is played on a board of sixty-four squares, eight on each side. The board is placed with a white square in the corner to the right of the player. There are sixteen men on each side, and they are placed as in the accompanying diagram.

DIAGRAM 1

As the reader may observe, the men are placed symmetrically, facing one another. Reading from left to right in the back row we have: Rook, Knight, Bishop, Queen, King, Bishop, Knight, and Rook. One Pawn is placed immediately in front of each of these pieces. The Rook and Knight on the King's side should be marked with a red mark to distinguish them from the Rook and Knight on the Queen's side. It is advisable to play on a board with buff and black squares or buff and green squares. The pieces should be of the so-called Staunton pattern and their base should be about two-thirds the size of the square. This combination will give the student an easy and clear sight of the board. The player having the white pieces begins the game. Each player moves alternately.

2. THE MOVES

The Rook

The Rook (indicated in chess notation by the letter R) moves in a straight line, on its rank or file, one or more squares at a time so long as there are not any of its own men in the way. The Rook cannot jump

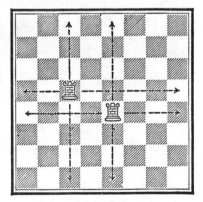

DIAGRAM 2

over any man. Should there be an opponent's man
in the way, the Rook may capture it by removing it
from the board and taking its place on the square
where the man stood. It is interesting to note that
because of the nature of the Rook's move, it commands the same number of squares no matter where
it is put. This does not occur with any of the other
pieces. (In the above Diagram the Rooks stand at
K 4 and Q B 5. The meaning of this will be seen
later in the chapter on notation.)

The Bishop

The Bishop (indicated in chess notation by the
letter B) moves on an oblique line, along the diagonals on which it stands, one or more squares at a
time, provided there is no obstruction on its way.
It cannot jump over another man, but should an opponent's man be in its way, it can take the man, occupying the square on which the man stood.

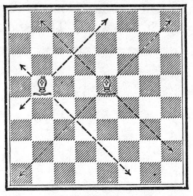

DIAGRAM 3

The B commands more or less squares according to
its position. In the diagram above, the B moving

along the white squares commands nine squares besides the one he stands on; the B moving along the
black squares four more squares than the other, or
thirteen in all, besides the one he stands on. As the
reader progresses, he will understand the importance
of these details. It should be noticed that because of
the nature of its movements a single B can move only
over 32 of the 64 squares of the board. When in
the centre of the board, however, it commands just
one square less than the Rook, which can move all
over the board.

The Queen

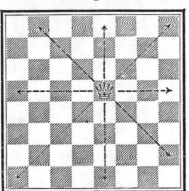

DIAGRAM 4

The Queen (indicated in chess notation by the letter Q) has the combined moves of the R and the B.
It can move to any square of the rank or file on which
it stands, or it can move to any of the squares along
the diagonals on which it stands. It can do so only
so long as there is no obstruction on its way. It cannot jump over another man. Should an opponent's
man be in its way, the Q can capture it, occupying
the square on which stood the opponent's man. When

in the centre of the board, as in the above diagram, the Q commands 27 squares besides the square on which it stands.   The Q is by far the most powerful piece of the whole game.

The Knight

The Knight (indicated in chess notation by Kt) moves in a rather peculiar way.   To explain the move of the Kt it may be best to refer to the diagram.

DIAGRAM 5

The Kt situated on the black square (Q 4) can move to any of the eight squares indicated by dots. This means that the Kt always moves from a white square to a black square, or *vice versa,* and never from white to white or from black to black.   It means that the Kt moves one square vertically or hori- zontally — North or South, East or West — and then one more square diagonally in the same general direc- tion.   For instance, if it moves vertically North, it will move North-East or North-West diagonally. The Kt commands more or less squares according to the position it occupies. Eight is the largest number of squares it can command at one time. It may capture any of the opponent's pieces that may be placed in any of the squares under its command. Because of the peculiar nature of its movement the Kt is the only piece that can jump over the other pieces, either of his side or of the opponent's. The Kt, like the Q and the R, can move over all the sixty-four squares. An interesting exercise is to try to move the Kt so as to cover all the sixty-four squares without going over the same square twice.

The King

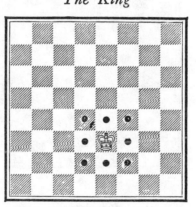

DIAGRAM 6

The King (indicated in chess notation by the letter K) moves one square at a time in any direction. In the accompanying diagram the King standing at K 3 can go to any of the squares marked with a dot. The King captures in exactly the same way as it moves. The King is the only piece that cannot move into a square commanded by any of the opponent's pieces. In consequence the King is never taken. Eight is the largest number of squares that the King may command at one time.

The Pawn

The Pawn (indicated in chess notation by the letter P) is the least valuable of all the men. The Pawn can move forward only, never backward and never sidewise. It moves forward on its file, one square at a time, except on the first move when it has the option of moving either one or two squares.

DIAGRAM 7

The pieces are set for the game to begin. In this position any Pawn can move either one or two squares, as indicated by the dots. The P in front of the Q has moved one square only. The P in front of the K has moved two squares, but once it has moved it can continue to move forward only one square at a time. It can do so if there is no piece in front of it to stop its march forward. The Pawn does not capture in the way it moves, and in this it differs from all the other pieces. It captures diagonally, as shown in the following diagram:

DIAGRAM 8
White to move

The White Pawn at K 4 can capture either one of the Black Pawns, but it cannot capture the Knight.

The Pawn has one more power. When it reaches the eighth rank it becomes, at the player's choice, any piece of its own colour except a King. Thus there may be a game with three or more Rooks, Knights, Bishops, or Queens on one side, but never more than one King. Since the Queen is the most valuable piece, when a Pawn reaches the eighth rank, it is generally exchanged for a Queen; hence the expression " Queening a Pawn." Thus the least important of all the men may occasionally become the most important of the whole lot.

3. CHECK AND CHECKMATE

When the King is attacked by a piece it is said that the King is in check. Now by the rules of the game the King must get out of check. The King may get out of check in three ways: by moving away from the line of action of the attacking piece, by capturing the attacking piece, or by interposing one of his own pieces between the King and the attacking piece. When the King is attacked in such a way that none of these three means of getting out of check is available, then it is said that the King is checkmated.

The object of the game is to checkmate the King, i.e. to check the King in such a manner that he has no way of getting out of check.

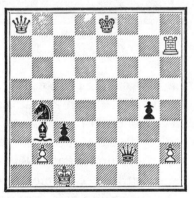

DIAGRAM 9
Black to move

In the above position White has won the game because the Black King has been checkmated. All the requisites are there: the King is in check by the action of the White Queen. This Q cannot be taken by any of the Black pieces, nor is there any Black piece which can be interposed between the checking Q and the checked King, and finally the five squares to which the King might move are all commanded either by the checking Q or the Rook standing at R 7.

4. STALEMATE

When a King *not* subjected to a check is in such a position that he cannot move without going into check, and at the same time there is no other piece which can be moved, then the King is said to be stalemated, and the game is drawn, i.e. neither side wins.

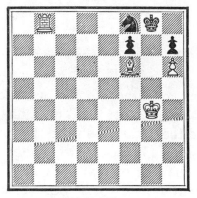

DIAGRAM 10
Black to move

In the position shown above, it is Black's turn to move. The Black King is not attacked, that is he is not in check. On the other hand he cannot move without going into check, which is not allowed by the rules of the game; nor can Black move the Kt, because it would uncover the King which would then be under check by the White Rook. Black is therefore in a stalemate position and the game is a draw.

5. CASTLING

Castling is a combined move which each player can make only once in a game and which is made jointly

DIAGRAM 11

by the King and either Rook. In order to make this move neither the K nor the R must have been moved before, and the squares between the two pieces must be free, as shown in the above diagram. Under those conditions the R is brought over next to the K, and the K is moved over to the other side of the R, as shown in the following diagram.

DIAGRAM 12

This is castling on the King's side, and the move should be made by taking and moving both pieces simultaneously. Under the conditions existing in the diagram, castling on the Queen's side would be impossible because the Q B is between the K and the R.

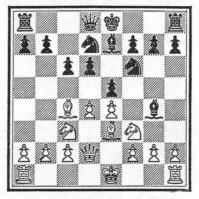

DIAGRAM 13

In the above diagram the squares are cleared between both the Rooks and the K, and therefore castling can take place as before or as shown in the diagram below.

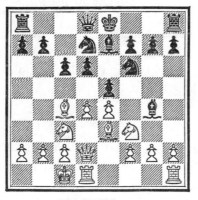

DIAGRAM 14

This is called castling on the Queen's side and in chess notation is written O – O – O, as against O – O for the K's side. The rules of the game do not permit castling while the K is in check, nor if the K or the castling R has been moved previously, nor while one of the squares over which the K must pass is under attack by an opponent's piece. For instance, castling is not permitted under the conditions of the diagram below.

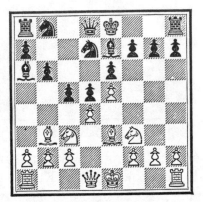

DIAGRAM 15
White to play

The reason is that the square K B is under the attack of the Black B at Q R 3. In all five diagrams, if it were Black's move, Black could castle on the King's side.

6. CHESS NOTATION

For the purpose of the study of the game and in order to facilitate the task of scoring and recording games, several systems of chess notation have been devised. Some are more scientific than others, but since we are not concerned with this aspect of the matter, we shall simply follow the so-called English

Notation. For this purpose it would be well to study closely the following diagram:

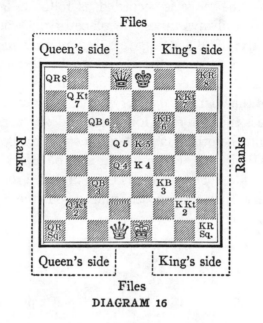

DIAGRAM 16

In the above diagram the Q and K are on their respective squares. All the pieces on the side of the Q are Queen's side pieces, and all the squares on the side of the Q are Queen's side squares. In the same way all the pieces on the side of the K are King's side pieces and all the squares on the side of the K are King's side squares. The horizontal lines are called ranks, lines, or rows, and the vertical lines are called files. The student should study the diagram closely in order to become familiar with the notation. For instance, the squares marked Q 4 and K 4, are Q 4 and K 4 for White, but those same squares are Q 5 and K 5 for Black, because one begins to count from

his own side. Thus if the pieces are set on their orig-
inal squares and White moves his King's Pawn two
squares the move is recorded as follows: P — K 4.
The dash always takes the place of the word " to."
Similarly, if Black answers by moving his King's
Pawn two squares, the move would be recorded as
P — K 4 because Black in his turn counts from his
side of the board. In other words, the fourth rank for
White is the fifth rank for Black and *vice versa*. The
files, on the other hand, are the same for both sides.
Thus White's K B file would also be Black's King's
Bishop file. The reason is evident, since the files are
named after the pieces placed on their original
squares.

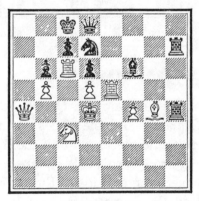

DIAGRAM 17

The above diagram would be recorded in notation
as follows: White: K at Q 4, Q at Q R 4, Rooks at
Q B 6 and K 5, Kt at Q B 3, B at K Kt 4, Pawns at
Q Kt 5, Q 5 and K B 4; Black: K at Q B sq., Q at Q
sq., Rooks at K R 2 and K R 5, Kt at Q 2, B at
K B 3, Pawns at Q Kt 3, Q B 2 and Q 3. The student

should look this over carefully and familiarize himself with the notation, for he will need this knowledge all through the book. There is one more sign; viz., an X which means " takes." Thus when a Pawn takes another Pawn we do not write " P takes P " but simply P X P. The same procedure is followed with all the pieces. When castling one must specify which side, and write thus: castles K's side or castles Q's side, according to the side of the board on which castling takes place. This is also written sometimes as follows: O — O for castling on the King's side and O — O — O for castling on the Queen's side. Both ways are in common use. Again we must stress the necessity for the student to know the subject thoroughly in order to follow the text. Later, as the student progresses, he should try to familiarize himself with other notations, the German and others, so that he may with ease follow the text of any annotated chess game, whether it be published in German or any other language. With one notation well in hand, the others can be learned without the slightest difficulty.

Notation Signs

K	stands for	King.
Q	" "	Queen.
R	" "	Rook.
Kt	" "	Knight.
B	" "	Bishop.
P	" "	Pawn.
X	" "	takes.
O — O	" "	castles on the King's side.
O — O — O	" "	castles on the Queen's side.

e.p.   stands for en passant (see below).
ch.   "   "   check.

In some text-books the following signs are used:
+ for better, — for inferior, = for equal.   In some
foreign texts a sort of a cross is used for check and a
double cross for checkmate.

Taking " en passant "

Now that the student is familiar with the notation
we will proceed with the one move purposely left out
so far, called taking " en passant," which is simply
French for taking " in passing."   In chess notation
these two words are indicated by e.p.

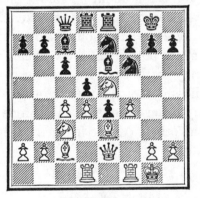

DIAGRAM 18
Black to play

In the above diagram, White's last move was to
advance his K B P two squares, from K B 2 to K B 4.
In so doing he has passed through the square K B 3
controlled by the Black Pawn at K 5.   Under such
conditions Black has the right to take the Pawn " en
passant " as indicated in the following diagram:

DIAGRAM 19
White to play

As the diagram shows, the result is the same as if White had only moved his B P one square and Black had taken it. Had Black decided not to take the Pawn e.p., he could no longer have taken it with his P at K 5; because according to the rules of the game the capture must be made at once, or the right to take e.p. is lost. Proper consideration will show that a capture e.p. can only take place by a P situated on the fifth rank and only against another P situated on the adjacent file; provided that the advancing Pawn has not been previously moved, and an attempt is made to move it two squares at a time. All these conditions must exist for such a move to take place. For instance had White's P been at K B 3 instead of K B 2, before it was moved to K B 4, no taking e.p. would be allowable. Taking e.p. is optional, not compulsory, but it must be done on the next move or the right to take is lost. Because of the difficulty involved in the comprehension of this move the student should go over the above explanations with care in order to make certain that he understands the move. Before proceeding any further the student should go over what has been written with regard to the moves of the pieces and the notation, and make sure that he is familiar with it.

Chapter II

THE WAY TO LEARN AND TO IMPROVE YOUR GAME

CHESS is easy to learn but difficult to play well. Order and method will do a great deal towards good play. The student should therefore go carefully over what has already been written. Once he is certain that he is familiar with the moves and the notation, he should practise by himself, placing the King in different mating positions. He should, for the purpose, use different pieces, increasing and decreasing their number, in order to master the action and power of the pieces against the King. This practice will develop the student's imagination and will make the game more interesting to him, thus increasing his desire to improve. It should be evident that the handling of a few pieces is easier than the handling of a larger number. For that reason we shall begin by giving a few simple mates and simple endings which will serve as a guide for the student. Once he learns and masters those endings, he should try to put up similar endings for himself, using his imagination for the purpose, and then try to solve those endings along the same lines as those given before. By such practice he ought to improve his game considerably.

The same kind of practice should be later used with the openings and the middle game. By constantly using and developing his imagination the player will not only improve his play, but will realize the beauties of the game and thereby increase his desire to master it. Throughout this practice it will be found easy to put the pieces in different positions apparently similar to those previously studied. What will be difficult will be to prove the positions to be of the same type, and to solve them along the same lines. It will be difficult to increase the number of pieces and yet handle them efficiently, since co-ordinating the action of the pieces is not only one of the most important things in chess, but also one of the most difficult. It is the enormous variety in chess which makes the game so difficult and also so interesting and so beautiful. The student will also find it difficult to avoid gross errors. He should not be discouraged thereby. Even the best players suffer from such lapses.

I. SIMPLE MATES

The first thing a student should do, is to familiarize himself with the power of the pieces. This can best be done by learning how to accomplish quickly some of the simple mates.

The ending Rook and King against King.

The principle is to drive the opposing King to the last line on any side of the board.

In this position the power of the Rook is demonstrated by the first move, R — R 7, which immediately confines the Black King to the last rank, and the mate is quickly accomplished by: 1 R — R 7, K — Kt 1; 2 K — Kt 2.

The combined action of King and Rook is needed to arrive at a position in which mate can be forced.

DIAGRAM 20

The general principle for a beginner to follow is to *keep his King as much as possible on the same rank, or, as in this case, file, as the opposing King.*

When, in this case, the King has been brought to the sixth rank, it is better to place it, not on the same file, but on the one next to it towards the centre.

2...K — B 1; 3 K — B 3, K — K 1; 4 K — K 4, K — Q 1; 5 K — Q 5, K — B 1; 6 K — Q 6.

Not K — B 6, because then the Black King will go back to Q 1 and it will take much longer to mate. If now the King moves back to Q 1, R — R 8 mates at once.

6...K — Kt 1; 7 R — Q B 7, K — R 1; 8 K — B 6, K — Kt 1; 9 K — Kt 6, K — R 1; 10 R — B 8 mate.

It has taken exactly ten moves to mate from the original position. On move 5 Black could have played K — K 1, and, according to principle, White would have continued 6 K — Q 6, K — B 1 (the Black King will ultimately be forced to move in

front of the White King and be mated by R — R 8);
7 K — K 6, K — Kt 1; 8 K — B 6, K — R 1;
9 K — Kt 6, K — Kt 1; 10 R — R 8 mate.

DIAGRAM 21

Since the Black King is in the centre of the board,
the best way to proceed is to advance your own King
thus: 1 K — K 2, K — Q 4; 2 K — K 3. As the
Rook has not yet come into play, it is better to advance the King straight into the centre of the board,
not in front, but to one side of the other King. Should
now the Black King move to K 4, the Rook drives
it back by R — R 5 ch. On the other hand, if 2 ...
K — B 5 instead, then also 3 R — R 5. If now
3 ... K — Kt 5, there follows 4 K — Q 3; but if instead 3 ... K — B 6; then 4 R — R 4, keeping the
King confined to as few squares as possible.

Now the ending may continue: 4 ... K — B 7;
5 R — B 4 ch, K — Kt 6; 6 K — Q 3, K — Kt 7;
7 R — Kt 4 ch, K — R 6; 8 K — B 3, K — R 7. It
should be noticed how often the White King has
moved next to the Rook, not only to defend it, but

also to reduce the mobility of the opposing King.
Now White mates in three moves thus: 9 R — R 4 ch,
K — Kt 8; 10 R — any square on the Rook's file,
forcing the Black King in front of the White,
K — B 8; 11 R — R 1 mate. It has taken eleven
moves to mate, and, under any conditions, I believe
it should be done in under twenty. While it may be
monotonous, it is worth while for the beginner to
practise such things, as it will teach him the proper
handling of his pieces.

Now we come to two Bishops and King against
King.

DIAGRAM 22

Since the Black King is in the corner, White can
play 1 B — Q 3, K — Kt 2; 2 B — K Kt 5, K — B 2;
3 B — B 5, and already the Black King is confined
to a few squares. If the Black King, in the original
position, had been in the centre of the board, or away
from the last row, White should have advanced his
King, and then, with the aid of his Bishops, restricted

the Black King's movements to as few squares as possible.

We might now continue: 3...K — Kt 2; 4 K — B 2. In this ending the Black King must not only be driven to the edge of the board, but he must also be forced into a corner, and, before a mate can be given, the White King must be brought to the sixth rank and, at the same time, in one of the last two files; in this case either K R 6, K Kt 6, K B 7, K B 8, and as K R 6 and K Kt 6 are the nearest squares, it is to either of these squares that the King ought to go. 4...K — B 2; 5 K — Kt 3, K — Kt 2; 6 K — R 4, K — B 2; 7 K — R 5, K — Kt 2; 8 B — Kt 6, K — Kt 1; 9 K — R 6, K — B 1. White must now mark time and move one of the Bishops, so as to force the Black King to go back; 10 B — R 5, K — Kt 1; 11 B — K 7, K — R 1. Now the White Bishop must take up a position from which it can give check next move along the White diagonal, when the Black King moves back to Kt 1. 12 B — K Kt 4, K — Kt 1; 13 B — K 6 ch, K — R 1; 14 B — B 6 mate.

It has taken fourteen moves to force the mate and, in any position, it should be done in under thirty.

In all endings of this kind, care must be taken not to drift into a stalemate.

In this particular ending one should remember that the King must not only be driven to the edge of the board, but also into a corner. In all such endings, however, it is immaterial whether the King is forced on to the last rank, or to an outside file, e.g. K R 5 or Q R 4, K 1 or Q 8.

We now come to Queen and King against King. As the Queen combines the power of the Rook and the Bishop, it is the easiest mate of all and should always be accomplished in under ten moves. Take the following position:

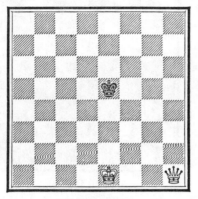

DIAGRAM 23

A good way to begin is to make the first move with the Queen, trying to limit the Black King's mobility as much as possible. Thus: 1 Q — B 6, K — Q 5; 2 K — Q 2. Already the Black King has only one available square 2...K — K 4; 3 K — K 3, K — B 4; 4 Q — Q 6, K — Kt 4. (Should Black play K — Kt 5, then Q — Kt 6 ch); 5 Q — K 6, K — R 5 (if K — R 4, K — B 4 and mate next move); 6 Q — K Kt 6, K — R 6; 7 K — B 3, K moves; 8 Q mates.

In this ending, as in the case of the Rook, the Black King must be forced to the edge of the board; only, the Queen being so much more powerful than the Rook, the process is far easier and shorter. These are the three elementary endings and in all of these

the principle is the same. In each case the co-operation of the King is needed. In order to force a mate
without the aid of the King, at least two Rooks are
required.

DIAGRAM 24
White to play

With two Rooks the process is simple. As usual
the King must be driven to the last line or rank.
Thus we begin by 1 R — K R 4, K — B 4; 2
R — Q R 5 ch, K — Kt 3. Now we cannot play
R — K R 6 ch, because the K would take the R. The
thing to do is to bring the R along the same rank
where it stands, as far away as possible from the K,
without putting it on the same file as the other R.
Thus we now play 3 R — Q Kt 4, K — B 3;
4 R — Kt 6 ch, K — K 2; 5 R — R 7 ch, K — Q sq;
6 R — Kt 8 ch mate.

The method followed in these endings is simple
and the student should find no trouble in learning the
proper procedure.

DIAGRAM 25

2. SIMPLE ENDINGS, PAWN PROMOTION

The gain of a Pawn is the smallest material advantage that can be obtained in a game; and it often is sufficient to win, even when the Pawn is the only remaining unit, apart from the Kings. It is essential, speaking generally, that *the King should be in front of his Pawn, with at least one intervening square.*

If the opposing King is directly in front of the Pawn, then the game cannot be won. This can best be explained by the following examples.

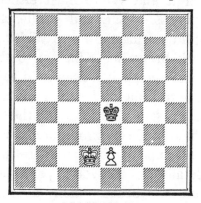

DIAGRAM 26

The position is drawn, and the way to proceed is for Black to keep the King always directly in front of the Pawn, and when it cannot be done, as for instance in this position because of the White King, then the Black King must be kept in front of the White King. The play would proceed thus: 1 P — K 3, K — K 4; 2 K — Q 3, K — Q 4. This is a very important move. Any other move would lose, as will be shown later. As the Black King cannot be kept close up to the Pawn, it must be brought as far forward as possible and, at the same time, in front of the White King.

3 P — K 4 ch, K — K 4; 4 K — K 3, K — K 3; 5 K — B 4, K — B 3. Again the same case. As the White King comes up, the Black King must be kept in front of it, since it cannot be brought up to the Pawn.

6 P — K 5 ch, K — K 3; 7 K — K 4, K — K 2; 8 K — Q 5, K — Q 2; 9 P — K 6 ch, K — K 2; 10 K — K 5, K — K 1; 11 K — Q 6, K — Q 1. If now White advances the Pawn, the Black King gets in front of it and White must either give up the Pawn or play K — K 6, and a stalemate results. If instead of advancing the Pawn White withdraws his King, Black brings his King up to the Pawn and, when forced to go back, he moves to K *in front* of the Pawn ready to come up again or to move in front of the White King, as before, should the latter advance.

The whole mode of procedure is very important and the student should become thoroughly conversant with its details; for it involves principles to be taken up later on, and because many a beginner has lost identical positions from lack of proper knowledge. At this stage of the book I cannot lay too much stress on its importance.

In this position White wins, as the King is in front of his Pawn and there is one intervening square.

DIAGRAM 27

The method to follow is to
advance the King as far as is compatible with the safety of the Pawn and never to advance the Pawn until it is essential to its own safety.
Thus:

1. K — K 4, K — K 3.

Black does not allow the White King to advance, therefore White is now compelled to advance his Pawn so as to force Black to move away. He is then able to advance his own King.

2. P — K 3, K — B 3; 3. K — Q 5, K — K 2.

If Black had played 3 . . . K — B 4, then White would be forced to advance the Pawn to K 4, since he could not advance his King without leaving Black the opportunity to play K — K 5, winning the Pawn. Since he has not done so, it is better for White not to advance the Pawn yet, since its own safety does not require it, but to try to bring the King still farther forward. Thus:

4. K — K 5, K — Q 2; 5. K — B 6, K — K 1.

Now the White Pawn is too far back and it may be brought up within protection of the King.

6. P — K 4, K — Q 2.

Now it would not do to play K — B 7, because Black would play K — Q 3, and White would have to bring back his King to protect the Pawn. Therefore he must continue.

7. P — K 5, K — K 1.

Had he moved anywhere else, White could have played K — B 7, followed by the advance of the Pawn to K 6, K 7, K 8; all these squares being protected by the King. As Black tries to prevent that, White must now force him to move away, at the same time always keeping the King in front of the Pawn. Thus:

8. K — K 6.

P — K 6 would make it a draw, as Black would then play K — B, and we would have a position similar to the one explained in connexion with Example 5.

8...K — B 1; 9 K — Q 7.

King moves and the White Pawn advances to K 8, becomes a Queen, and it is all over.

This ending is like the previous one, and for the same reason should be thoroughly understood before proceeding any further.

3. TWO PAWNS AGAINST ONE PAWN

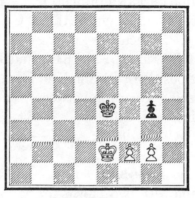

DIAGRAM 28
White to play

The kind of ending shown in the diagram is apt to occur either in the form shown above or in a similar form. Sometimes there may be three Ps against two, or four Ps against three. Sometimes the Ps may all be on one side of the board, or again they may be on both sides.

When the Pawns are on one side of the board only, as in the above diagram, the procedure is always the same, and consists in exchanging one of White's Pawns for Black's Pawn in such a way as to bring about a similar position to that in Diagram 27 where White's King can move forward in such a way as to obtain a winning position. Except in those endings where one of the two Pawns is on the Rook's file, two Pawns against one will win in almost every case. In the position in above diagram if White plays 1 P — K B 3 ch, the game will be a draw because Black will play P × P and then keep his K always in front of the Pawn in the way shown in the first part of this section on Pawn promotion. White, however, may easily avoid such a thing by playing first 1 P — Kt 3. If then K — Q 5, 2 P — B 3, P × P; 3 K × P followed by K — Kt 4 and K — R 5, obtaining the position with the K in front of the P with one intervening square in between, which, as already shown, wins. If after 1 P — Kt 3, K — K 4; 2 K — K 3, K — B 4; 3 K — Q 4, K — B 3; 4 K — K 4, K — Kt 4; 5 K — K 5, K — Kt 3; 6 K — B 4, K — R 4; 7 K — B 5, K — R 3; 8 K × P and with two Pawns for nothing White will have no trouble to Queen one of them. If after 1 P — Kt 3, K — B 4;

DIAGRAM 29
White to play

then K — Q 3, so that if Black now plays K — K 4 White may play K — K 3 and get exactly the same position as played before. The reason for White's second move K — Q 3 is based on the laws governing the " Opposition," a matter which will be discussed in the second part of the book. At present it is too early to discuss this matter, but its importance must be apparent from the example just given. The student may also realize the great importance of the handling of the King. No smaller advantage can be obtained than that of a Pawn, but when there is almost nothing left on the board, the game can be won by the proper handling of the King.

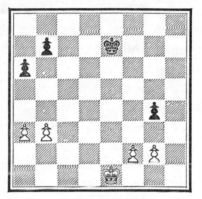

DIAGRAM 30
White to play

When the Pawns are on both sides of the board, as in the diagram shown above, the procedure is easier. First we bring up the King to the Pawns in order to insure their safety, then advance the Pawn that is free from opposition — that is, the Pawn that has not another Pawn opposing it — thus obtaining a so-called passed Pawn; and then, through a policy of " blocking " and " attrition," we get the desired results. This latter policy will be very easily under-

stood by following the text. Thus, 1 K — K 2, K —
K 3; 2 P — B 3, P × P; 3 K × P (it is always best
to have the free Pawn as far away from the others
as possible), K — B 4; 4 P — Kt 4 ch, K — Kt 4.
Now the " blocking " process can be started on the
other side. 5 P — Kt 4, P — Kt 3; 6 P — R 4, K —
Kt 3; 7 K — B 4, K — B 3; 8 P — Kt 5 ch, K —
Kt 3. Once more White may safely advance on the
Queen's side to finish the " blocking " process, 9 P —
Kt 5. It is better to advance the Kt P so that in case
Black decides to exchange, the Pawns left will remain
on the Kt's file. (The Rook's P is the only P that
cannot be Queened against the King, no matter how
many intervening squares there may be between the
King in front of the P and the P itself.) 9...P —
R 4. The " blocking process " is now finished, and
the process of " attrition " begins. 10 K — Kt 4,
K — Kt 2; 11 K — B 5, K — B 2; 12 P — Kt 6 ch,
K — Kt 2; 13 K — Kt 5, K — Kt sq; 14 K — B 6,
K — B sq; 15 P — Kt 7 ch, K — Kt sq. The process of " attrition " is now ended.

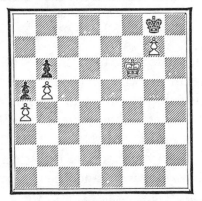

DIAGRAM 31
White to play

White cannot continue with 16 K — Kt 6 because it would result in " stalemate," which as already stated makes the game a draw; but White can now abandon the single Pawn and run quickly with his K to the other side of the board to take the two defence-less Black Pawns. Thus: 16 K — K 6, K × P; 17 K — Q 6, K — B 2; 18 K — B 6 followed by K × P and K × P, and with two Ps for nothing White will have no trouble in Queening one of them.

It is time now for the student to review what has been written before in order to make certain that everything is thoroughly understood. Then he should, by himself, out of his own imagination, put up different Pawn endings similar to those explained above. No other practice will give him a better idea of the value of time in chess than these King and Pawn endings. It should be borne in mind that a player strong in the endings will have a decided advantage over the others. The champions of the world for the last eighty years have had, as a characteristic of their skill, extraordinary ability in end-game playing.

4. RELATIVE VALUE OF THE PIECES

Before going on to the general principles of the openings, it is advisable to give the student an idea of the proper relative value of the pieces. There is no complete and accurate table for all of them, and the only thing to do is to compare the pieces separately.

For all general theoretical purposes the Bishop and the Knight have to be considered as of the same value, though it is my opinion that the Bishop will prove the more valuable piece in most cases; and it is well known that two Bishops are almost always better than two Knights.

The Bishop will be stronger against Pawns than the Knight, and in combination with Pawns will also be stronger against the Rook than the Knight will be.

A Bishop and a Rook are also stronger than a Knight and a Rook, but a Queen and a Knight may be stronger than a Queen and a Bishop.

A Bishop will often be worth more than three Pawns, but a Knight very seldom so, and may even not be worth so much.

A Rook will be worth a Knight and two Pawns, or a Bishop and two Pawns, but, as said before, the Bishop will be a better piece against the Rook.

Two Rooks are slightly stronger than a Queen. They are slightly weaker than two Knights and a Bishop, and a little more so than two Bishops and a Knight. The power of the Knight decreases as the pieces are changed off. The power of the Rook, on the contrary, increases.

The King, a purely *defensive* piece throughout the middle game, becomes an *offensive* piece once all the pieces are off the board, and sometimes even when there are one or two minor pieces left. The handling of the King becomes of paramount importance once the end-game stage is reached.

Chapter III

THE OPENINGS FROM ELEMENTARY
POINT OF VIEW

THE opening is the beginning of the game, as the word indicates. A sound beginning is often the key to a good ending. The openings pave the way for what is to follow and the result of the game may hinge on the first half-dozen moves. Because the thirty-two pieces are involved, the opening is naturally the most difficult part of the game, and thousands of books have been written on its technical aspects. Beginners, however, should not go too deeply into the technical aspects of the thing, but merely look into it from a general point of view. This will be the line of procedure in the present book. For the more advanced player, as well as the expert, there are several chapters in " Chess Fundamentals " covering the essential points. The technical works on the subject are intended only for the experts or for those who wish to become experts at the game.

From an elementary point of view the openings mean the bringing into action of the pieces by both sides. The centre Pawns should be advanced, in order to make room for the Bishops and the Queen. When once these pieces and the Knights have been moved and brought into action, and the squares between the Rooks and the King have been cleared, castling may take place; and finally by bringing the Rooks towards the centre and putting them on the open files we have the whole force of each side in action. All this should be done in from eight to twelve moves, and to get it done while hampering the opponent at the same time is the crux of the matter. If a player succeeds in obtaining full development for all of his forces ahead of his opponent, he may feel fully satisfied with his work. This should outweigh any other consideration in the student's mind. We shall now proceed with the elementary general theory of the game.

For theoretical purposes, the game is divided into three parts: the opening, the middle game, and the end game. In the opening, the beginner should strive for a quick development, posting his pieces offensively but with due regard for their safety. The opening should be completed within ten or twelve moves and care should be taken not to lose a single Pawn in the process. Should the opponent offer any material, even a Pawn, which in your estimation you may capture without danger, it is advisable to take the offered piece, even if as a result full development is retarded for one or two moves. If as a result of the capture full development will be retarded more than two moves, then it is doubtful whether the capture should be made. It might be risked with the White pieces but never with the Black, except on very rare occasions. No definite rule can be given in such matters. The player must use his own judgement and he must also consider the type of opponent he is pitted against. Castling should generally be done on the King's side, because it is usually safer, but no material or positional advantage should be sacrificed on that account.

I am giving below examples to illustrate these points.

White		Black
P — K 4	1	P — K 4

With this move, both White and Black open the way for the Queen and one of the Bishops. There is only one other move, viz: P — Q 4, that will have the same effect, and therefore we must consider these two moves as the two best opening moves.

Kt — K B 3	2	Kt — Q B 3

White brings out a Kt and at the same time attacks Black's P; while Black defends the P and develops a piece at the same time. It should be borne in mind that whenever we speak of pieces we mean only the big pieces, like Bishops, Knights, Rooks and Queens, and not the Pawns or the Kings which are invariably designated by their own names.

B — Kt 5	3	

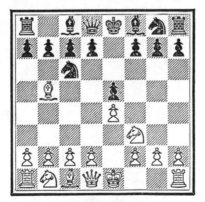

DIAGRAM 32
Black to play

This constitutes the Ruy Lopez, one of the oldest, soundest and best of all the openings. There are now several ways for Black to proceed. We shall take one at random.

	3	Kt — B 3
Castles	4	

Black should now proceed with his development either by playing B — K 2 or P — Q 3, but should not take the proffered Pawn, which is a Grecian gift. Were Black to capture the P, White would play P — Q 4 and thereby obtain a great advantage in development which would finally bring him back his P with interest.   Another example:

White		Black
P — K 4	1	P — K 4
Kt — K B 3	2	B — B 4

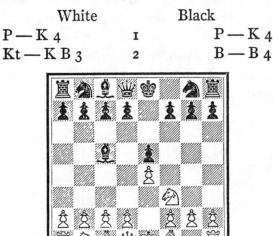

DIAGRAM 33
White to play

Black offers a Pawn hoping to gain time for development in case White should take it.   In accord with the theory explained above White should take it because it will retard his development only one or two moves. In all such cases the thing for the player to consider is what the immediate danger is, and if he sees none he should take the P and face the consequences. Very often experience alone will teach him when to take and when to decline.

Let us look now at a Queen's Pawn opening.

P — Q 4   1   P — Q 4

With the advance of this P the way is opened for both the Q and the B. The difference from the previous opening is that the P is defended, which is not the case when the K's P is advanced. This is one argument in favour of considering this the strongest opening. For the time being, however, that argument is beyond the scope of the present book. We must for our purpose consider P — Q 4 as no better than P — K 4.

Kt — K B 3   2   Kt — K B 3

Following the general rule both sides bring out their K's Kt.

P — Q B 4   3

This constitutes the Q's Gambit. Experience has shown that it is advisable to make this move. In fact, in all Queen's side openings, if White's intention is to play his Q's Kt to Q B 3, it has been found best to play P — Q B 4 first. When it is the intention to play the Q Kt to Q 2 then it is not necessary to make the other move first. It is true that White offers a P apparently for nothing, but experience has shown that Black cannot hold the P without danger. We now have an example of one of the principles enun-

DIAGRAM 34
Black to move

ciated above, i.e. that White can afford to offer a Pawn if in so doing he gains one or two moves in development, and also that Black should take the gift provided he is not retarded too much in his own development.

	3	P × P
Kt — B 3	4	B — B 4

Black wants to get his pieces out as quickly as possible in accord with the general theory explained before. It should be noticed that White could have regained his P immediately by Q — R 4 ch followed by Q × P, but he is in no hurry to do so because it will retard his development. Besides, it is generally bad policy to bring out the Q so early in the game, before the smaller pieces are out and doing something.

P — K 3	5	P — K 3
B × P	6	B — K 2
O — O	7	O — O

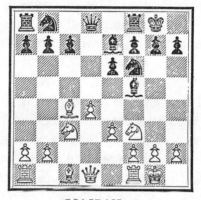

DIAGRAM 35
White to move

The game is now well on its way. The opening has not followed the well-known classical lines to be found in many a text-book, but rather the simple general system expounded in the present volume. Later on, in the second part of this book, we shall see that we have not deviated far from the straight and narrow path. In fact, only against experts would the general development be found deficient, and that on Black's side, and only because of certain idiosyncrasies of this opening beyond the scope of this book. The main thing for the reader to realize is the general way in which the game is gradually developed, bringing out first the Kt then the B, then once more a Kt or a B and then castling, the Q being kept back. The Q, being the most valuable piece, should not be brought out without proper support. She needs the smaller pieces to protect her or to help her in her work.

Let us now consider certain further things with regard to the openings. The squares K 4, Q 4, K 5 and Q 5 are the centre squares. They are of the greatest importance for the general theory of the game and especially of the openings. Control of the centre is essential for a complete and sound development. Control of the centre is also essential, during the middle game, for any successful attack against the King; and finally, breaking up the enemy's centre is one of the strategical advantages to work for, both in the opening and in the middle game. Incidentally, this shows the close relation between the opening and the middle game. Some of the principles of the openings are also principles of the middle game, and in the same manner some of the principles of the middle game are principles of the end game also.

Coming back to the openings we find that most of the gambits (i.e. openings in which a Pawn is offered) have as one of their main objects the aim of breaking up the opponent's centre. Take the Queen's Gambit for example. The play is as follows: 1 P — Q 4, P — Q 4; 2 P — Q B 4. Apart from any other consideration, White tries to induce Black to take the Pawn in order to have a preponderance of force in the centre. By eliminating the Black Pawn at Q 4, White obtains the control of the centre. With the King's Gambits it is the same. The play is as follows: 1 P — K 4, P — K 4; 2 P — K B 4. Again a Pawn is offered in order to draw away Black's P at K 4 and thus obtain control of the centre. With the above principle in mind let us now look at another opening.

P — K 4	1	P — K 4
Kt — K B 3	2	Kt — Q B 3
B — B 4	3	B — B 4

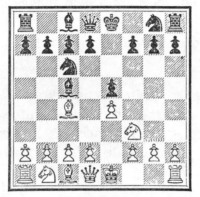

DIAGRAM 36
White to play

This is called the " Giuoco Piano," Italian words which mean " slow game." The name of the opening is probably due to the fact that the development is methodical and easy on both sides.

O — O	4	Kt — B 3
P — Q 3	5	P — Q 3
B — K 3	6	B — Kt 3

Black could have taken the B, but on retaking White would have his centre reinforced by the P at K 3. To have doubled Pawns is usually a disadvantage, but in the openings, when the Pawn is doubled towards the centre, there is a compensation that often outweighs the disadvantage of the doubled Pawn. In this particular case there is a further consideration, namely that in doubling the Pawn, Black would open a file for the White Rook at K B, thus bringing into action a very powerful piece that was doing nothing. From the above it is evident that the balance of opinion would be for the text move, as opposed to B × B.

Q Kt — Q 2	7	O — O
P — B 3	8	B — K 3

Black repeats White's manœuvre. The situation, however, is not the same, since White's game is now fully developed, and furthermore he has already prepared an advance against Black's centre through his last move, P — B 3.

Q B × B	9	R P × B
B × B	10	P × B
Q — Kt 3	11	Q — Q 2
P — Q 4	12	P × P
P × P	13	

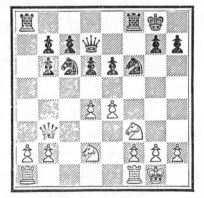

DIAGRAM 37
Black to play

The opening is over. White has obtained control of the centre, but Black's position is solid; White has a little more freedom for his pieces, but Black has two open files for his Rooks while White has only one, the Q B file. All things considered, White has a slight advantage of position, but probably not enough to win. With proper playing the White side should always obtain a slight advantage of position, because of the first move which gives him the initiative, and to have the initiative is always an advantage. With this example the discussion of the opening is over for the first part of the book.

THE MIDDLE GAME

In the middle game, the player should strive for combinations leading to a direct attack against the King, whenever possible. This is not exactly the point of view of the expert, who will conspire for positional or material advantage of any kind, irrespective of whether the attack is made against the King or any other piece, but the beginner should practise mostly combinations involving attacks against the King. It will bring him more enjoyment because of the type of game involved, and at the same time it will give him very much needed practice for the day when he will reach a more advanced stage. In making a direct attack against the King, or in building up the combinations leading to such an attack, the beginner should not hesitate to sacrifice material to the extent of a Pawn, or even a Knight or Bishop; but he should be extremely careful if the sacrifice involves as much as a Rook, to say nothing of the Queen, since these

pieces can be sacrificed only when there is an immediate mate to follow; otherwise the chances of success are practically zero.

I give below some illustrations covering these
points.

DIAGRAM 38
White to play

This is a simple position. The material is the same
on both sides, but White has the advantage of having
taken possession of the open file, and also of having
the Q and B placed in an attacking position against
the K. If it were Black's move he could quickly
equalize the game by playing either Kt — K 4 or one
of the Rooks to Q sq. It is therefore evident that
White must anticipate this by playing 1 P — K 5. If
now Black takes the P with the Kt, then 2 Kt × Kt,
B × Kt; 3 Q — R 7 ch, K — B; 4 R — Q 7 and
mate follows since Black can prevent the check at
R 8 only by advancing his K Kt P and then White
would play Q × B P mate. This is a very simple case,
and of course Black should not have taken the P
offered by White. But let us go back to the diagram

and assume that Black plays the best move. Then we have 1 P — K 5, P — Kt 3; 2 Q — K 4, Q R — Q; 3 Q — K B 4, and White has an excellent attack against the King. In fact I am inclined to think that with proper playing White should evolve a win from that position. At present, however, the student should not concern himself with this aspect of the subject, but only with the way to work his pieces into an attacking position. In the next examples we shall go deeper into the matter.

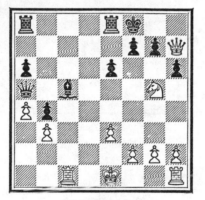

DIAGRAM 39
White to play

The above example is taken from a game Capablanca-Schroeder played at the end of 1915 in the Rice Memorial Tournament. It is given to show that the safest course is not always the best, and that very often it pays to be enterprising. The beginner is not expected to play accurately, but it is his style that we are concerned with at present; hence the insistence upon showing positions to be won by direct and violent attacks against the King. In the position of

the diagram White could have played safely as fol-
lows: 1 Kt — K 4, B — Kt 3 (best); 2 R — B 6,
Q — K B 4 (much the best. Any other move would
give White an easy win.) 3 Q × Q, P × Q; 4 Kt —
Q 6, K R — Kt; 5 Kt × P at B 4, R — B; 6 R × R,
R × R; 7 K — Q 2.

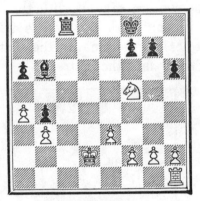

DIAGRAM 40
Black to play

To prevent R — B 7 and to make room at the same
time for the Rook, so that if Black plays R — B 6
White can answer with R — Q Kt defending the
Pawn. The result of all this would be an ending with
a Pawn ahead, and to be sure White could win with
proper play; but it would take some time and a great
deal of care. Instead of all this, White played for
the attack as follows (go back to diagram 39):
1 Q — R 8 ch, K — K 2; 2 Q × Kt P, P × Kt;
3 Q × Kt P ch, K — Q 3. (The K has to go to the
protection of the B and thus becomes exposed to the
attack of all the White pieces.) 4 K — K 2,
Q R — B; 5 R — B 4, K — B 3. Black wants to go

over to safety with his K while he has a chance.
6 K R — Q B, K — Kt 3. Now everything is safe
for Black, for the moment, but White takes advantage of the fact that all the Black pieces are
" pinned " or " blocked ": that is, the Black Q cannot move at all, the K cannot move without losing
the B and the R at Q B cannot leave the defence of
the B, nor can the B move because it will lose a R.
Black's pieces can now be said to be fixed, and with
plenty of time White begins advancing his free Pawn
so as to take it to the eighth row and Queen it. Thus
7 P — R 4,

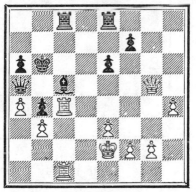

DIAGRAM 41
Black to play

7...P — B 4; 8 Q — Kt 7 (in order to come back to
K 5, keeping Black's pieces tied up and exerting the
maximum of pressure; and also protecting the square
R 8, where the P is going to Queen). 8...R — K 2;
9 Q — K 5, R — B 3. A gross error, but Black's
game was hopeless. 10 R × B and Black resigns,
because if he plays R × R White will answer
11 Q — Q 6 ch, King moves; 12 R × R attacking the

Q and the other R will also go. But suppose that we go back to the diagram, and that Black instead of 7...P — B 4 had played his best move 7...R — B 2, then we should have 8 P — R 5, K R — Q B; 9 P — R 6, B — Q 3. This is the only place where the B can go without losing a R. 10 Q × Q ch, K × Q; 11 R× R, R × R. (Not B × R because then R — B 6 will paralyse all the Black pieces.) 12 R × R, B × R.

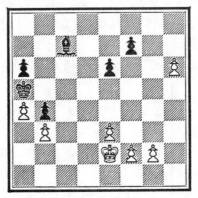

DIAGRAM 42
White to play

Now we have a most interesting situation. Black has come out of the battle ahead in material, but his K is over on the Q's side, while the issue is going to be decided on the K's side; and in an end game, with practically no pieces on the board except Pawns, it is generally fatal to have the K away from the scene of action. White must now try to Queen his Pawn before Black can bring his King over. Therefore he plays: 13 P — B 4, B — Q. (White wants to play P — R 7 and then Queen the Pawn. Black tries to prevent it by placing his B at B 3 where it commands

the sq K R 8 of White.) 14 P — Kt 4, B — B 3;
15 P — Kt 5, B — R sq; 16 P — K 4, K — Kt 3.
The King begins to move over to the K's side; unfortunately he is too far and cannot arrive in time.
17 P — B 5, P × P; 18 P × P, K — B 4; 19 P —
Kt 6, P × P; 20 P × P and Black has no defence
against 21 P — Kt 7. This shows how an apparently
dull game may suddenly become very lively and exciting. It shows also the great importance of the element of time in the endings, and the important part
that the King plays in the end games, sometimes as
a defensive piece, and at other times as an attacking
piece. The whole example, while not so valuable to
the expert, is most useful to the average player, because it involves a number of general principles that
the student should always bear in mind.

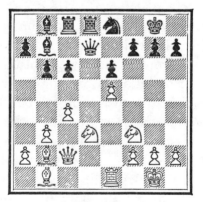

DIAGRAM 43
White to play

Let us analyse the above situation in the light of
what has gone before. The material is even except
for the fact that Black has a R for a Kt. That is already a decided advantage; more than enough to win,

provided there be no immediate danger. But with
regard to *position* the spectacle changes at once.
Black has taken the open file by putting both his Q
and his R on it. White blocks the immediate action
by the position of his Kt at Q 3; but that is purely
defensive and if there were no other compensation the
preponderance of material on Black's side would decide the issue. White, however, has the move, and
the rest of his pieces are better posted than Black's.
He can therefore take advantage of the element of
time as well as of the element of position. Let us
consider further the position of the pieces on both
sides. Black has his two Bishops blocked, one by
the White Pawn at K 5 and the other by his own
Pawn at Q B 3. His R at Q B is doing nothing at
present and needs time to be manœuvred into a position of attack or defence. His Kt at K sq is in a
purely defensive position. Yet the fact that it is
the one piece placed defensively near the K makes the
position good from a defensive point of view, and the
advantage of material on his side makes this a point
rather in Black's favour. The one bad feature of the
position of Black's Kt is that it blocks the moves of
his own pieces and prevents them from going over to
the defence of the King. All in all, a look at the board
will show that Black's position is cramped. If it were
Black's move, he could relieve his position considerably by playing P — Q B 4, and at the same time begin an attack. By that move he would threaten
B × Kt, breaking up White's King's side and reduc-
ing the attacking forces of White. The chances are
that, notwithstanding everything else to the contrary,
this would be sufficient to decide the game in Black's

favour. It is therefore needful for White to prevent the advance of that Pawn.

Let us look now to the White side of the question. All of White's pieces are fairly well posted. With the exception of the B at Q Kt sq all the pieces have plenty of mobility and can be quickly shifted from one side of the board to the other. Furthermore the B at Q Kt supports the Q in the masked attack against the Black King, an attack which will develop as soon as the Kt at Q 3 is moved forward. This completes the general survey of the position and from it we gather that there are two main objects to consider: viz., to prevent the advance of Black's Q B P and to move forward White's Kt at Q 3. The first object could be easily accomplished by P — B 5. This would be a good move but rather slow in its effect, and the chances are that by skilful defence Black might get out without losing the game. The second object could be accomplished by moving the Kt to Kt 4, B 4 or B 5. The first move would leave the Kt alone on the Q's side, doing nothing. It would therefore be a bad move. The second move would bring the Kt over to the attack on the K's side and would therefore be, from a general point of view, an excellent move. Black, however, by playing P — Kt 3, would be able to defend the position and possibly to escape from disaster. The third move, Kt — B 5, is the one that accomplishes the desired object. It blocks the advance of Black's Q B P, and by attacking the Q it prevents Black from defending the attack on his K. It is true that the Kt is given up, but we have already recommended such tactics whenever there is a chance of success. Let us see what

would happen: 1 Kt — B 5, P × Kt; 2 Q × P ch,
K — B.

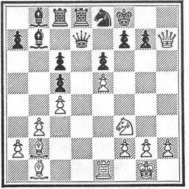

DIAGRAM 44
White to move

White can already do as he pleases. He can draw
the game by perpetual check, since after Q — R 8 ch,
K — K 2; Q — R 4 ch, Black could do nothing better than to go back with his K to B sq, and thus
White could keep on checking for ever. Under these
conditions White can now consider whether or not
there is something better to do, and he finds that by
playing B — R 3 he will get back all his material
with interest. Thus 3 B — R 3, B — Q 3. This is
the only way to avoid immediate disaster, for Black
cannot stand B × P ch by White. 4 P × B (R — Q
sq would also win, but it would lead to more complications; and once the game is won the best procedure
is to finish in the simplest way in order to avoid the
chance of errors) 4...Kt × P (Q × P would be no
better); 5 B × P, K — K 2; 6 Kt — K 5, Q — K;
7 R — Q, Q — R; 8 Q × Q, R × Q; 9 R × Kt,
K R — Q;

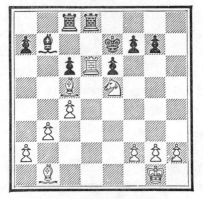

DIAGRAM 45
White to move

10 R — Q 7 ch, K — B 3 (if K — K, 11 R — K 7 ch,
followed by R × B ch); 11 R × P ch, K — Kt 4 (if
K × Kt, P — B 4 ch mate); 12 B — K 3 ch, K —
R 5; 13 R — B 4 ch, K — R 4; 14 B — Kt 6 ch,
K — Kt 4; 15 P — R 4 ch, K — R 3; 16 R moves to
any square and it is checkmate by the B at K 3. The
position has been carried to the very end so that the
student may see what co-ordination of the action of
the pieces will do. Co-ordinating the action of the
pieces is the main feature of the middle game, especially when carrying a direct attack against the King.
With this example we leave, for the time being, the
middle game, and pass on to the end game, where the
time element is often of paramount importance.

THE END GAME

In the ending, the element of time is of great importance. Material also counts for more, because
with the lesser number of pieces the percentage represented by a single Pawn is much greater. The King,

which during the opening- and middle-game stage is often a burden because it has to be defended, becomes in the end game a very important and aggressive piece, and the beginner should realize this, and utilize his King as much as possible. In end games where Kings and Pawns only are left on the board the King should usually be marched forward to the centre of the board. Even in endings where Rooks or small pieces only are involved, the King often should be marched forward toward the centre. The beginner is generally afraid to utilize his King for such purposes and is therefore handicapped when facing a more experienced opponent. The fact is that many endings are decided by the respective positions of the Kings or the ability of the Kings to march forward toward the centre of the board. The beginner should therefore practise along these lines at every opportunity. In doing so, he will find the game more exhilarating and at the same time he will be marching along the road to success.

The following illustrations cover these points.

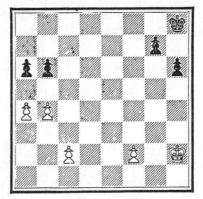

DIAGRAM 46
White to move

In the above position, White wins because the Black King is one square too far from the Q's side Pawns. Were the Black King at K Kt instead of K R, or were Black to move first, so that he could play K — Kt before White started to advance his Pawns, the ending would be in favour of Black, although, with skilful playing on White's part, the game would probably be a draw. All this shows clearly the importance of the element of time in the endings. In fact it is only the move that decides the issue, not the position nor the material; since the material is equal on both sides and the position is rather in favour of Black (because of the fact that the Black forces are well balanced on both sides of the board, while the White forces are not). In order for the position to be considered even, all of White's Pawns would have to be on the Queen's side, so that the preponderance of material on that side would be large enough to offset the advantage of the equally balanced force on Black's side. This point is brought up because of its importance in the general discussion of the strategy and tactics of the game. It will come up again in the second part of the book.

Going back to the position in the diagram, we find that the way to win is as follows: 1 P — Q B 4, K — Kt; 2 P — B 5, P × P; 3 P — Kt 5. This is the point of the whole thing. If White retakes the Pawn, Black arrives on time with his King. By advancing the P, White goes to Q on the Kt's file, one square farther away from the Black King, and that is enough to win. 3 ...P × P; 4 P × P. White could also play P — R 5, Queening the Pawn one square farther still from the Black King; but this is not necessary, and since it would leave Black with a larger force it should not be done. 4...K — B; 5 P — Kt 6, K — K; 6 P — Kt 7, Queening on the next move and winning easily. Take another example:

DIAGRAM 47
White to move

In the above position it is again possession of the move that wins for White. This time the position and forces are practically balanced on both sides. The fact that Black's Pawns on the King's side are united is an advantage, but too small in this case to be of any consequence. The position of the White Pawns on the Q's side is offensively an advantage, but defensively a disadvantage. Offensively the Pawns are strongest the farther away they are from their base of operation; defensively they are strongest the nearer they are to that base. What decides the issue in this ending is the respective positions of the Kings. With the move, Black by playing K — Kt would be in a position to meet the rush of the White

King, but without the move, he will be helpless in a short time. Thus: 1 K — B 3, K — Kt; 2 K — K 4, K — B 2; 3 K — Q 5, K — K 2; 4 K — B 6 and White will win the two Black Pawns for nothing. In this example is shown the important part that the King can play in an end game, as well as the importance of the element of time; since having the move, that is, being one move ahead (which is being one time ahead) is what decides the issue.

It will be convenient now to call attention to the fact that because of the nature of the chess board and of the way the K moves, the square Q R 8 marked on the following diagram can be reached by the White King in the same number of moves no matter where, on the bottom rank, the K may be placed.

DIAGRAM 48

Whether the White K be placed as in the diagram, or at any of the squares Q R, Q Kt, Q B, Q, K, K B or K Kt, he will take exactly the same number of moves to reach the square marked Q R 8. Similarly in the following diagram

DIAGRAM 49

both the Kings can reach the square marked Q B 6 in the same number of moves. Accuracy as to the time it takes for the K to reach a given square is of the utmost importance in the end game. King and Pawn endings occur very frequently, and therefore the student would do well to become proficient in them: it will score many a game for him.

Let us now look at endings where Rooks are involved.

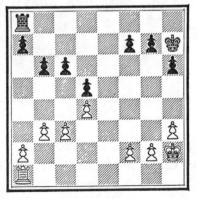

DIAGRAM 50
White to move

In the above diagram, once more, having the move decides the issue. The position of the pieces is exactly alike on both sides. It is the time element alone that counts. Whoever moves first plays R — K and obtains a winning game. Thus: 1 R — K, K — Kt 3; 2 R — K 7, P — Q B 4; 3 P × P, P × P; 4 R — Q 7 and White wins a Pawn; usually sufficient to win the game among players of the same strength, provided they have learned how to handle their King.

Let us look now at an example where the King is used in conjunction with the Rook.

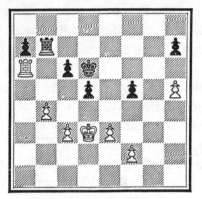

DIAGRAM 51
White to play

In the above diagram the material is even, but White has an advantage in position. The Black R cannot leave the second line because White will then take the Q R P. Furthermore, as soon as the Black R leaves the Q Kt file, White will be able to play P — Q Kt 5, threatening to win a Pawn. Black in fact has not very much to do except to mark time and wait for White. With all this, White could not win if it were not because of the intervention of his own K. Thus the way to proceed is as follows: 1 K — Q 4, P — R 3; 2 P — K B 4. This forces Black to move either his R or his K. He can move his K only to Q 2 or Q B 2 because of his Q B P, and then White would play K — K 5 winning the K B P. He must, therefore, move his R. 2 . . . R — K 2; 3 P — Kt 5, R — Q B 2. Black could also play R — K 5 ch, but then, after K — Q 3 for White, he would have to play R — B 5 to defend his Q B P, bringing about very much the same position as in the text. 4 P × P (not R × P ch, because of R × R, P × R, K × P and Black with his passed P on the Q R file would have an excellent chance of winning the game). 4 . . . R × P. If the K moved to K 3, White would play K — B 5, and if the R moved anywhere on the second row, White would play P — B 7 ch, winning at least one more P. 5 R × P, R — B 5 ch. To drive back the King. 6 K — Q 3, R — B 2. White threatened to play R — K R 7 winning the P at R 3. 7 R — R 8. White could also win by exchanging the Rooks and bringing about a K and P ending similar to those already shown in this chapter, but the text move is more accurate, and is made with the object of showing the combined action of R and K. 7 . . . R — K R 2. White threatened to play R — R 8 winning the P at R 3. 8 K — Q 4, K — K 3; 9 R — K 8 ch, K — Q 3; 10 R — Q 8 ch, and White wins the Q P; and with two Pawns to the good he should have no trouble in winning the game.

Chapter IV

MAIN RULES AND ETHICS OF THE GAME

THERE are several chess codes. The international code, generally used, is based mainly on the revised edition of the British code. Those who wish to know the rules used in International and Championship contests should obtain the code from any bookseller. For general purposes, however, the following rules should prove sufficient.

1. Any piece that is touched must be moved. If it cannot be moved there is no penalty.

2. Moves must not be taken back. If a gross mistake is made and the game is lost thereby, there is only one thing to do — to resign gracefully and begin a new game.

3. Do not hover over the pieces too much. It is unethical and it leads to errors. The celebrated German Master, Dr. Tarrasch, used to sit with his hands under his thighs to avoid hesitation and to keep from moving hastily. It is not bad to move quickly, but it is bad to move hastily.

4. When playing a match to decide a wager or to find out who is the better player, a time limit should be set for a number of moves. Between twenty and thirty moves per hour is a fairly slow speed. The World's Championship is played at the rate of forty moves in two and a half hours. The leading players, on the other hand, when playing for amusement, take about ten or fifteen minutes per game. The average

player will naturally take longer, probably between thirty and fifty minutes per game.

5. No warning need be given when attacking an opponent's piece, but check to the King must be respected. It is therefore convenient to announce check when it takes place.

6. No move is completed until the piece is put on a square and the hand leaves the piece. If after putting a piece on a square and before taking your hand off it you find that the move is a mistake, you are entitled to another move with the same piece, but the piece must be moved. If the move involves the capture of an opponent's piece, and you have already touched the opponent's piece, either with your hand or with the moving piece, then the piece must be taken with the piece you have in your hand. The only condition under which you can be released from that obligation will be that the move you intended to make is illegal. In that case you will still be compelled to move the piece you touched if it is possible at all.

CHESS MAXIMS

1. Do not hover over the pieces. It prevents clear thinking.

2. In the openings, bring your pieces out quickly, and castle early in the game, generally on the King's side. Castling usually makes the position of your King safer.

3. In the endings, when the Queens have been exchanged, and one or two minor pieces only are left with the Pawns, bring your King out toward the centre of the board. Also advance your Pawns

quickly. Pawn endings are won, as a rule, only by Queening a Pawn. Often victory goes to the swift.

4. Co-ordinate the action of your pieces. Sporadic raids with single pieces are usually fatal against an alert opponent. Also it is generally advisable, especially early in the game, to keep your Pawns together.

5. Train yourself to move quickly but deliberately, never hastily.

6. Play an aggressive game, unless you find from experience that your temperament makes you totally unfit for it. Take the initiative at every opportunity. To have the initiative is an advantage.

7. In the openings bring out one Kt at least before bringing out the Bishops.

8. Put your Rooks on the open files.

9. Play combinations at every opportunity in order to develop your imagination.

10. Never hesitate to make a move for fear of losing. Whenever you think a move is good go ahead and make it. Experience is the best teacher. Bear in mind that you may learn much more from a game you lose than from a game you win. You will have to lose hundreds of games before becoming a good player.

11. In the openings avoid moving the same piece twice. It retards your development. Also move pieces in preference to Pawns.

12. Take every Pawn or piece that may be offered to you unless you see immediate danger.

Note: — The reader should bear in mind that these

maxims are not absolutely certain rules, infallible in every case, but rather a sort of general guide. In the main, however, they are correct. Good players follow them and it takes an expert to know when to deviate from them.

Part Two

Introduction

THE varied and intricate combinations which often
keep the beginner from plunging into the mysteries of
the game are the very things that charm the average
chess player most. An attack involving the sacrifice
of one or more pieces, if successfully carried out, ap-
peals strongly to his imagination and urges him on in
quest of its mysteries. In following his natural bent
for the unknown, however, the player often neglects
the plain facts and fundamental principles which he
must observe if he is to obtain his results through
brilliant combinations. In considering all these
things, it should be borne in mind that while the
tactics may change according to the circumstances,
the fundamental strategical principles are always the
same.

As already stated in the first part of the book, the
game of chess, for the purpose of study and theory,
has been divided in three parts: the opening, the middle game, and the end game. The opening deals with
the process of bringing into action the different pieces.
The middle game deals with that of using these pieces
to obtain a definite result, and the end game is the
final stage where the combined efforts of the opening
and the middle game may bring about a satisfactory
decision. We are speaking here, of course, of a well-
fought game where no gross error has been made nor
any fundamental principle violated by either side.
When either side commits a gross error or violates a

fundamental principle, the game is likely to end quickly. Among experts, some games have ended right in the opening, because a gross error made by one side gave the opponent such an advantage that it was thought useless to continue. A good many contests have ended in the middle game because, through some fault committed by one side, the other player has been able to work up a devastating attack which has produced either a mate or such an advantage of material as to make it futile to continue. In obtaining these results the masters have, at times, evolved many very beautiful combinations, which have been the delight of generations of chess players. The normal thing, however, among experts, is for the contest to be decided in the end game after a hard struggle.

Most text-books deal with the openings, and in a highly technical way that is more or less useful to the expert but not of much value to the average player. The same might be said of most of the books on the end game. Hardly anything has been written on the middle game. The middle game does not lend itself to purely technical discussion. Only the very best players could write interestingly on the subject, and the leading players have seldom shown an inclination to discuss their methods. A discussion of these methods would be most interesting to those in quest of supremacy.

What to do. What to avoid

For the purpose of study there are very few books to be recommended to the average players. Those few books are written along general lines; the proper method, in my opinion, of approaching the subject. That method is the one followed in this book. The plan to follow for those who wish to improve their game is to take such a book as a guide, learn the general principles and follow the general lines of the text; then practice, practice, and more practice. Play with better players whenever possible, and when playing against inferior players give them a small handicap so that you may be compelled to exert yourself in order to win. As a handicap you may give the odds of a draw (i.e. any drawn game to count as a win for your opponent), alternating the move, or you may give the odds of a draw and the move. You may also give the odds of Pawn and move, and in that case the K B P is the Pawn to be given, because any other Pawn would give a compensation in development which might easily upset the given advantage. When you give odds of Pawn and move, your opponent always takes the White pieces and moves first. White's best move under such conditions is P — K 4. You may also give the odds of a Kt. In that case you always have the White pieces and move first. You may give either Kt, but it is the general custom to give the Q Kt. Do not attempt to give bigger odds. It unbalances your forces too much and cannot be good for your game. When playing against experts take any odds that may be offered to you, and remember never to lose courage because you do not win. Remember that the greatest of players have lost hundreds of games in their time.

In trying to improve your game there is, to be sure, no better way than to take lessons from an expert, but those lessons should seldom be of a purely techni‧cal character.   Never be content simply to learn a series of moves by heart, in the openings or elsewhere, but strive to find the reasons for each move in the series.   As you improve, I recommend the method of study and practice I have followed in this book and in my " Chess Fundamentals "; for in these two vol‧umes I have done my best to guide the player ac‧cording to the wisest principles.

The way to improve

Once you have become a proficient player, it will be time to study or go over some of the many books on the openings in order to become familiar with the very large number of variations in every opening.   I refer to books of purely technical character.   But once more I must insist on the fact that such knowl‧edge is only useful to the expert.   You can play a very pretty game without any such knowledge, and the fact is that the author himself never studied such books in his life and only when he was already one of the leading players did he occasionally take a look at them; and then more out of curiosity than anything else.   With regard to this there are two anecdotes that may be interesting to the reader.   At San Sebas‧tian International Masters Tournament of 1911, which I won, I was playing one day against the cele‧brated Dr. Tarrasch, a master who had always made a very thorough study of the openings.   He was sup‧posed to have an excellent technical knowledge of any opening he played.   He had the White pieces and played a variation of the Giuoco Piano that I had never seen before. I played according to my ideas of general development and after some ten or twelve moves the Doctor began to think. He took a very long time to make his next move. It seems that up to this point I had been making the best moves of the opening according to the recognized authorities, but that then I had made a move not in the books, with the result that instead of getting the best of the game the Doctor was getting the worst of it. This prompted the comment from him after the game that not only did I know the books thoroughly but that I had improved on them. The fact was that I did not know a single book on the openings at the time but I had merely played on general lines according to the same principles I am expounding in this book.

On another occasion, while in Havana I received an invitation to play in a big International Tournament and I replied accepting the offer. I had not played at all for over a year and felt a little out of touch with the game. I thought that probably some new ideas had come up with regard to the technical side of the openings, and that it would be a good thing for me to know something about them. I inquired and obtained a recent book which contained most of the main lines of play of the openings, most in vogue at the time, together with the latest developments. I went through the book only to find to my great disappointment that it was of no use to me. I found not only what I considered tactical errors but what was far more important, I found also what to me seemed very serious strategical errors which might prove fatal in a game when facing a first class master.

There are besides some interesting books of various kinds that are very useful to the expert or near-expert. One of the most interesting is Reti's " Masters of the Chess Board." I refer only to the part written by Reti himself. He died before the book was finished and someone else wrote the last part of the book, which cannot be compared with the first. There are also books and publications dealing with problems and endings. Solving problems is good exercise for the imagination, and as such to be recommended. But problem positions are mostly positions of an artificial nature, not to be encountered in a real game and therefore not so useful as they would be if the positions were natural ones likely to occur in a game. Solving endings is about the most useful form of exercise, because the positions used are likely to occur in actual play; and the imagination has to be used as much in solving an end game as in solving a problem. Furthermore there is the question of accuracy. To solve an end-game problem or composition, accuracy is required, and accuracy is a valuable quality in a chess player. End-game compositions are often only reproductions of similar occurrences in actual games, and ability to solve such problems is a very valuable asset. Too much stress cannot be put on this point.

Let us now return to the study of certain endings and the principles involved therein.

Classical Endings

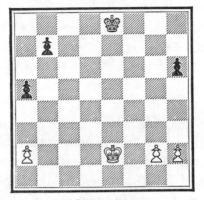

DIAGRAM 1
White to move

In the position in the diagram the forces are even. There is very little left; three Pawns and the King on each side. White's King is nearer the centre of the board, an advantage according to the principles explained previously in the text. White's Pawns are on a line with themselves and with their King. That makes their position sound, other things being equal. The Pawns are on the second line, an advantage defensively but a disadvantage offensively. All in all, White's position is perfectly solid. Now let us look at the Black side. Black's King is behind his Pawns and farther away from the centre than White's King. This is a disadvantage. Black's Pawns are not in line, also a disadvantage. Black's Pawns are forward as compared to White's, a disadvantage defensively but an advantage offensively. All in all, Black's position lacks the balance of White's position and therefore cannot be as good, all other things being equal. All this is from a theoretical point of view. From the practical side the fact is that if it were Black's move he could defend himself successfully by advancing his King towards the centre, towards the side where he has the superior force, namely the Q's side; and by following with the advance of his backward Q Kt P to Q Kt 4 in line with his Q R P. Thus by acting quickly on the side where he has the preponderance of material and by taking advantage of the better offensive position of his Pawns, Black could offset the advantage of White's better balanced position. It is White's move, however, and he obtains a winning position by his first move: 1 P — Q R 4. This move makes it impossible for Black to align his Pawns at the same time that it prevents their advance. This move involves one of the most valuable principles in chess, *a unit that holds two*. In other words, with a force of one you are holding a force of two. After the first move the procedure is comparatively simple, thus: 1...K — Q 2; 2 K — Q 3, K — B 3; 3 K — B 4, P — R 4. Black finds his advance blocked on the Q's side and therefore tries to create on the other side a similar situation. 4 P — Kt 3. This is the second key move in this ending, and in making it White follows once more one of the principles previously laid down for such situations — namely, to advance the Pawn that is free from opposition. If White played instead 4 P — R 4, Black could draw by playing P — Kt 3, and if White played 4 P — R 3 Black would actually win by playing P — R 5. The student would do well to work all this out by himself. The ending is very simple, and yet there is much variety to it and many fundamental principles involved. The element of time is seen here also in one of its many aspects. Let us continue: 4...P — Kt 3. Black can do nothing but mark time. 5 P — R 3, K — Q 3; 6 K — Kt 5, K — B 2; 7 P — Kt 4 and while the Black King is held to his Pawns, White will go on to Queen. If Black attempts to move his K to the K's side to stop the Pawn, White will then take both of Black's Q's side Pawns and then Queen his own Pawn.

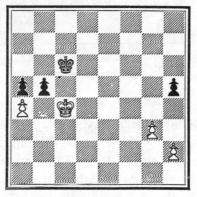

DIAGRAM 2
White to play

Now suppose that on his fourth move Black had played P — Kt 4 ch, instead of P — Kt 3, we should have then: 5 P × P ch, K — Kt 3; 6 P — R 3, P — Q R 5; 7 P — Kt 4, P × P; 8 P × P, P — R 6; 9 K — Kt 3, K × P; 10 P — Kt 5 and the White P cannot be stopped from Queening. If we dwell so long on this kind of ending and insist so much on its discussion, it is because of its importance and the importance of the principles involved.

This " type " of ending occurs frequently. Not

long ago one of the youngest masters, Eliskasses of
Austria, had the following ending:

DIAGRAM 3
White to move

Again the forces are even, and in fact if it were
Black's move he would have a very satisfactory position after P — Q Kt 4, straightening up his Pawn
line on the Q's side. It is White's move, however,
and he proceeds immediately to apply the principles
laid down in this book as follows: 1 P — Q R 4, to
hold back the backward Q Kt P of Black. Observe
how closely this procedure is similar to that of the
previous example. The whole thing hinges on the
fact that White is able to prevent or check the advance of Black's Q's side Pawns, while Black will not
be able later on to prevent a similar advance of White's
K's side Pawns. Victory will go to the player who
will be able to act with more freedom where he holds
the preponderance of force.

Let us go back to the diagram. 1 P — Q R 4,
K — B 3; 2 K — Q 3, P — Q Kt 4. White can win

by playing P × P ch followed by K — B 3 or by playing first K — B 3. The reader should work all this
out for himself. He will find it both useful and
entertaining. He should bear in mind that if Black at
any time plays P — K Kt 4 White can answer with
P — K Kt 4. The general procedure in any case will
be to play first P — K B 3 to be followed by P — K 4
and so on. The point is that in order to capture the
one Pawn, Black will have to leave the Q's side and
White will then be able to take both of Black's Q's
side Pawns and then Queen his own Pawn on that
side. But suppose now that instead of Black playing 1 ... K — B 3 he had played 1 P — Q B 5.

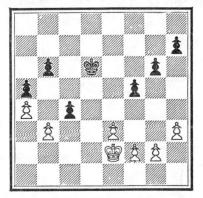

DIAGRAM 4
White to play

The procedure would then be: 2 P × P, K — B 4;
3 K — Q 3, K — Kt 5; 4 P — B 3, K × P;
5 K — B 3. This move prevents the King from
coming out immediately in order to advance his free
R's P. 5...P — Q Kt 4; 6 P — K 4, P — Kt 5 ch;
7 K — Kt 2, P — Kt 6; 8 P — K 5 and there is no
way to stop the K's P from Queening.

The endings given above are of a " type " which occurs rather frequently. There is one point to be considered at once, and that is the Pawn formation. The reader will have noticed that most of the trouble came from the backward position of one of the Pawns. The Pawn formation is very important at times. The Pawns are best generally when in line with each other. When advancing them a diagonal form should be kept as much as possible but never, if possible, a " V "-shaped formation. A " V "-shaped formation always leaves a backward Pawn, making it possible for one Pawn to stop two. Also during the early and middle-game stages a " V "-shaped formation permits a piece to be placed in between the Pawns absolutely safe from the attack of a Pawn. We shall revert to this matter of Pawn formation later when dealing with the openings.

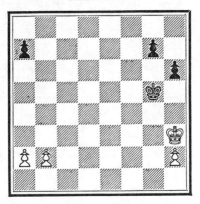

DIAGRAM 5
White to play

In the position shown above, White can draw by playing P — Kt 4 according to the general rule that governs such cases, i.e. *to advance the Pawn that is free from opposition.* But suppose that White, either because he does not know this principle or because he does not, in this case, sufficiently appreciate the value of its application; suppose, we say, that he plays 1 P — Q R 4. Then Black can win by playing 1 ... P — Q R 4, applying one of the cardinal principles of the high strategy of chess —

A unit that holds two

In this case one Pawn would hold two of the opponent's Pawns. The student cannot lay too much stress on this principle. It can be applied in many ways, and it constitutes one of the principal weapons in the hands of a master.

The example given should be sufficient proof. We give a few moves of the main variation: —

1.	P — R 4	P — Q R 4
2.	K — Kt 2	K — B 5
	(Best; see why.)
3.	P — Kt 4	P × P (Best.)
4.	P — R 5	P — Kt 6
5.	P — R 6	P — Kt 7
6.	P — R 7	P — Kt 8 (Q)
7.	P — R 8 (Q)	Q — K 5 ch
8.	Q × Q	K × Q

This brings the game to a position which is won by Black, and which constitutes one of the classical endings of King and Pawns. I shall try to explain the guiding idea of it to those not familiar with it.

I. A CLASSICAL ENDING

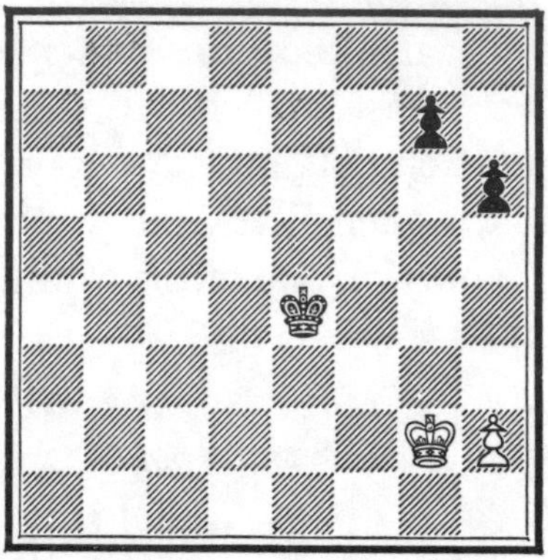

DIAGRAM 6   White to play

In this position White's best line of defence consists in keeping his Pawn where it stands at R 2. As soon as the Pawn is advanced it becomes easier for Black to win. On the other hand, Black's plan to win (supposing that White does not advance his Pawn) may be divided into three parts. The first part will be to get his King to K R 6, at the same time keeping intact the position of his Pawns. (This is all important, since, in order to win the game, it is essential at the end that Black may be able to advance his rearmost Pawn one or two squares according to the position of the White King.)

| 1. K — Kt 3 | K — K 6 |
| 2. K — Kt 2 | |

If 2 K — Kt 4, K — B 7; 3 P — R 4, P — Kt 3 will win.

| 2. .... | K — B 5 |
| 3. K — B 2 | K — Kt 5 |

4. K — Kt 2   K — R 5
5. K — Kt 1   K — R 6

The first part has been completed.

DIAGRAM 7   White to play

The second part will be short and will consist in advancing the R P up to the K.

6. K — R 1   P — R 4
7. K — Kt 1   P — R 5

This ends the second part.

DIAGRAM 8   White to play

The third part will consist in timing the advance of the Kt P so as to play P — Kt 6 when the White King is at R 1. It now becomes evident how necessary it is to be able to move the Kt P either one or two squares according to the position of the White King, as indicated previously. In this case, as it is White's move, the Pawn will be advanced two squares since the White King will be in the corner, but if it were now Black's move the Kt P should only be advanced one square since the White King is at Kt 1.

8.	K — R 1	P — Kt 4
9.	K — Kt 1	P — Kt 5
10.	K — R 1	P — Kt 6
11.	P × P	

If K — Kt 1, P — Kt 7.

11.	....	P × P
12.	K — Kt 1	P — Kt 7
13.	K — B 2	K — R 7

and wins.

It is in this analytical way that the student should try to learn. He will thus train his mind to follow a logical sequence in reasoning out any position. This example is excellent training, since it is easy to divide it into three stages and to explain the main point of each part.

The next subject we shall study is the simple opposition, but before we devote our time to it I wish to call attention to two things.

2. OBTAINING A PASSED PAWN

When three or more Pawns are opposed to each other in some such position as the one in the following diagram, there is always a chance for one side or the other of obtaining a passed Pawn.

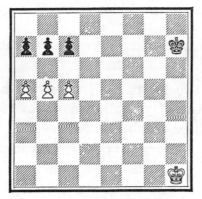

DIAGRAM 9

In the above position the way of obtaining a passed Pawn is to advance the centre Pawn.

1. P — Kt 6	R P × P

If B P × P; P — R 6,

2. P — B 6	P × B P
3. P — R 6	

and as in this case the White Pawn is nearer to Queen than any of the Black Pawns, White will win. Now if it had been Black's move Black could play

1.	P — Kt 3
2. B P × P	B P × P

It would not be advisable to try to obtain a passed Pawn because the White Pawns would be nearer to Queen than the single Black Pawn.

$$3. \ P \times P \qquad\qquad P \times P$$

and the game properly played would be a draw. The student should work this out for himself.

3. HOW TO FIND OUT WHICH PAWN WILL BE FIRST TO QUEEN

When two Pawns are free, or will be free, to advance to Queen, you can find out, by counting, which Pawn will be the first to succeed.

DIAGRAM 10

In this position whoever moves first wins.

The first thing is to find out, by counting, whether the opposing King can be in time to stop the passed Pawn from Queening. When, as in this case, it cannot be done, the point is to count which Pawn comes in first. In this case the time is the same, but the Pawn that reaches the eighth square first and becomes a Queen is in a position to capture the adversary's Queen when he makes one. Thus:

1. P — R 4   P — K R 4
2. P — R 5   P — R 5
3. P — Kt 6   P × P

Now comes a little calculation. White can capture the Pawn, but if he does so, he will not, when Queening, command the square where Black will also Queen his Pawn. Therefore, instead of taking, he plays:

4. P — R 6   P — R 6
5. P — R 7   P — R 7
6. P — R 8 (Q), and wins.

The student would do well to acquaint himself with various simple endings of this sort, so as to acquire the habit of counting, and thus be able to know with ease when he can or cannot get there first. Once again I must call attention to the fact that a book cannot by itself teach how to play. It can only serve as a guide, and the rest must be learned by experience, and if a teacher can be had at the same time, so much the faster will the student be able to learn.

4. THE OPPOSITION

When Kings have to be moved, and one player can, by force, bring his King into a position similar to the one shown in the following diagram, so that his adversary is forced to move and make way for him, the player obtaining that advantage is said to have *the opposition*.

DIAGRAM 11

Suppose in the above position White plays

    1. K — Q 4

Now Black has the option of either opposing the passage of the White King by playing K — Q 3 or, if he prefers, he can *pass* with his own King by replying K — B 4. Notice that the Kings are directly opposed to each other, and the number of intervening squares between them is odd — one in this case.

DIAGRAM 12

The opposition can take the form of Diagram 11, which can be called actual or close frontal opposition; or the form of Diagram 12, which can be called actual or close diagonal opposition, or, again, this form:

DIAGRAM 13

which can be called actual or close lateral opposition.

In practice they are all one and the same. The Kings are always on squares of the same colour, there is only one intervening square between the Kings, and the player who has moved last " *has the opposition.*"

Now, if the student will take the trouble of moving each King backwards as in a game in the same frontal, diagonal or lateral line respectively shown in the diagrams, we shall have what may be called *distant* frontal, diagonal and lateral opposition respectively.

The matter of the opposition is highly important, and takes at times somewhat complicated forms, all of which can be solved mathematically; but, for the present, the student should only consider the most simple forms. (An examination of some of the examples of King and Pawns endings already given will show several cases of close opposition.)

In all simple forms of opposition, *when the Kings are on the same line and the number of intervening squares between them is even, the player who has the move has the opposition.*

DIAGRAM 14

The above position shows to advantage the enormous value of the opposition. The position is very simple. Very little is left on the board, and the position, to a beginner, probably looks absolutely even. It is not the case, however. *Whoever has the move wins.* Notice that the Kings are directly in front of one another, and that the number of intervening squares is *even.*

Now as to the procedure to win such a position. The proper way to begin is to move straight up. Thus:

1.	K — K 2	K — K 2
2.	K — K 3	K — K 3
3.	K — K 4	K — B 3

Now White can exercise the option of either playing K — Q 5 and thus passing with his King, or of playing K — B 4 and prevent the Black King from passing, thereby keeping the opposition. Mere counting will show that the former course will only lead to a draw, therefore White takes the latter course and plays:

4.	K — B 4	K — Kt 3

If 4...K — K 3; 5 K — Kt 5 will win.

5.	K — K 5	K — Kt 2

Now by counting it will be seen that White wins by capturing Black's Knight Pawn.

The process has been comparatively simple in the variation given above, but Black has other lines of defence more difficult to overcome. Let us begin anew.

1.	K — K 2	K — Q 1

Now if 2 K — Q 3, K — Q 2, or if 2 K — K 3, K — K 2, and Black obtains the opposition in both cases. (When the Kings are directly in front of one another, and the number of intervening squares between the Kings is *odd*, the player who has moved last has the opposition.)

Now in order to win, the White King must advance. There is only one other square where he can go, B 3, and that is the right place. Therefore it is seen that in such cases when the opponent makes a

so-called waiting move, you must advance, leaving a
rank or file free between the Kings.   Therefore we
have —

2. K — B 3   K — K 2

Now, it would be bad to advance, because then Black,
by bringing up his King in front of your King, would
obtain the opposition.   It is White's turn to play a
similar move to Black's first move, viz.:

3. K — K 3

which brings the position back to the first variation
shown.   The student would do well to familiarize himself with the handling of the King in all examples of
opposition.   It often means the winning or losing of
a game.

5. THE RELATIVE VALUE OF KNIGHT AND BISHOP

Before turning our attention to this matter it is
well to state now that *two Knights alone cannot mate,*
but, under certain conditions of course, they can do
so if the opponent has one or more Pawns.

DIAGRAM 15

In the position of Diagram 15 White cannot win, although the Black King is cornered, but in the following position, in which Black has a Pawn,

DIAGRAM 16

White wins with or without the move. Thus:

    1. Kt — Kt 6   P — R 5

White cannot take the Pawn because the game will be drawn, as explained before.

    2. Kt — K 5   P — R 6
    3. Kt — B 6   P — R 7
    4. Kt — Kt 5   P — R 8 (Q)
    5. Kt — B 7 mate

The reason for this peculiarity in chess is evident. *White with the two Knights can only stalemate the King, unless Black has a Pawn which can be moved.*

Although he is a Bishop and a Pawn ahead the following position cannot be won by White.

DIAGRAM 17

It is the greatest weakness of the Bishop, that when the Rook's Pawn Queens on a square of opposite colour and the opposing King is in front of the Pawn, the Bishop is absolutely worthless. All that Black has to do is to keep moving his King close to the corner square.

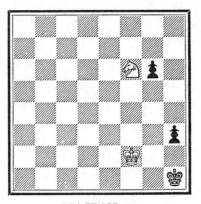

DIAGRAM 18

In the above position White with or without the move can win. Take the most difficult variation.

1.	K — R 7
2. Kt — Kt 4 ch	K — R 8
3. K — B 1	P — Kt 4
4. K — B 2	P — R 7
5. Kt — K 3	P — Kt 5
6. Kt — B 1	P — Kt 6 ch
7. Kt × P mate	

Now that we have seen these exceptional cases, we can analyse the different merits and the relative value of the Knight and the Bishop.

It is generally thought by amateurs that the Knight is the more valuable piece of the two, the chief reason being that, unlike the Bishop, the Knight can command both Black and White squares. However, the fact is generally overlooked that the Knight, at any one time, has the choice of one colour only. It takes much longer to bring a Knight from one wing to the other. Also, as shown in the following diagram, a Bishop can stalemate a Knight; a compliment which the Knight is unable to return.

DIAGRAM 19

The weaker the player the more terrible the Knight is to him, but as a player increases in strength the value of the Bishop becomes more evident to him, and of course there is, or should be, a corresponding decrease in his estimation of the value of the Knight as compared to the Bishop. In this respect, as in many others, the masters of today are far ahead of the masters of former generations. While not so long ago some of the very best amongst them, like Pillsbury and Tchigorin, preferred Knights to Bishops, there is hardly a master of today who would not completely agree with the statements made above.

DIAGRAM 20

This is about the only case when the Knight is more valuable than the Bishop.

It is what is called a "*block position*," and all the Pawns are on one side of the board. (If there were Pawns on both sides of the board there would be no advantage in having a Knight.) In such a position Black has excellent chances of winning. Of course, there is an extra source of weakness for White in having his Pawns on the same colour-squares as his

Bishop. This is a mistake often made by players. The proper way, generally, in an ending, is to have your Pawns on squares of opposite colour to that of your own Bishop. When you have your Pawns on squares of the same colour the action of your own Bishop is limited by them, and consequently the value of the Bishop is diminished, since the value of a piece can often be measured by the number of squares it commands. While on this subject, I shall also call attention to the fact that it is generally preferable to keep your Pawns on squares of the same colour as that of the opposing Bishop, particularly if they are passed Pawns supported by the King. The principles might be stated thus:

When the opponent has a Bishop, keep your Pawns on squares of the same colour as your opponent's Bishop.

Whenever you have a Bishop, whether the opponent has also one or not, keep your Pawns on squares of the opposite colour to that of your own Bishop.

Naturally, these principles have sometimes to be modified to suit the exigencies of the position.

DIAGRAM 21

In the position of Diagram 21 the Pawns are on one side of the board, and there is no advantage in having either a Knight or a Bishop. The game should surely end in a draw.

Now let us add three Pawns on each side to the above position, so that there are Pawns on both sides of the board.

DIAGRAM 22

It is now preferable to have the Bishop, though the position, if properly played out, should end in a draw.

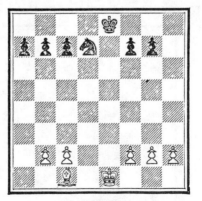

DIAGRAM 23

The advantage of having the Bishop lies as much in its ability to command, at long range, both sides of the board from a central position as in its ability to move quickly from one side of the board to the other.

In the position of Diagram 23 it is unquestionably an advantage to have the Bishop, because, although each player has the same number of Pawns, they are not balanced on each side of the board. Thus, on the King's side, White has three to two, while on the Queen's side it is Black that has three to two. Still, with proper play, the game should end in a draw, though White has somewhat better chances.

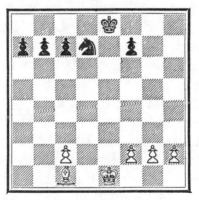

DIAGRAM 24

Here is a position in which to have the Bishop is a decided advantage, since not only are there Pawns on both sides of the board, but there is a passed Pawn (K R P for White, Q R P for Black). Black should have extreme difficulty in drawing this position, if he can do it at all.

DIAGRAM 25

Again Black would have great difficulty in drawing this position.

The student should carefully consider these positions. I hope that the many examples will help him to understand, in their true value, the relative merits of the Knight and Bishop. As to the general method of procedure, a teacher, or practical experience, will be best. I might say generally, however, that the proper course in these endings, as in all similar endings, is: Advance of the King to the centre of the board or towards the passed Pawns, or Pawns that are susceptible of being attacked, and rapid advance of the passed Pawn or Pawns as far as is consistent with their safety.

To give a fixed line of play would be folly. Each ending is different, and requires different handling, according to what the adversary proposes to do. Calculation by visualizing the future positions is what will count.

6. HOW TO MATE WITH A KNIGHT AND A BISHOP

Now, before going back again to the middle game and the openings, let us see how to mate with **Knight and Bishop**, and, then, how to win with a Queen against a Rook.

With a Knight and a Bishop *the mate can only be given in the corners of the same colour as the Bishop.*

DIAGRAM 26

In this example we must mate either at Q R 1 or K R 8. The ending can be divided into two parts. Part one consists in driving the Black King to the last line. We might begin, as is generally done in all such cases, by advancing the King to the centre of the board:

1. K — K 2   K — Q 2

Black, in order to make it more difficult, goes towards the white-squared corner:

2. K — Q 3   K — B 3
3. B — B 4   K — Q 4

4. Kt — K 2	K — B 4
5. Kt — B 3	K — Kt 5
6. K — Q 4	K — R 4
7. K — B 5	K — R 3
8. K — B 6	K — R 2
9. Kt — Q 5	K — R 1

The first part is now over; the Black King is in the white-squared corner.

DIAGRAM 27

The second and last part will consist in driving the Black King now from Q R 8 to Q R 1 or K R 8 in order to mate him. Q R 1 will be the quickest in this position.

10. Kt — Kt 6 ch	K — R 2
11. B — B 7	K — R 3
12. B — Kt 8	K — R 4
13. Kt — Q 5	K — R 5

Black tries to make for K R 1 with his King. White has two ways to prevent that, one by 14 B — K 5,

K — Kt 6; 15 Kt — K 3, and the other which I give
as the text, and which I consider better for the student to learn, because it is more methodical and more
in accord with the spirit of all these endings, *by using
the King as much as possible.*

14.	K — B 5!	K — Kt 6
15.	Kt — Kt 4	K — B 6
16.	B — B 4	K — Kt 6
17.	B — K 5	K — R 5
18.	K — B 4	K — R 4
19.	B — B 7 ch	K — R 5
20.	Kt — Q 3	K — R 6
21.	B — Kt 6	K — R 5
22.	Kt — Kt 2 ch	K — R 6
23.	K — B 3	K — R 7
24.	K — B 2	K — R 6
25.	B — B 5 ch	K — R 7
26.	Kt — Q 3	K — R 8
27.	B — Kt 4	K — R 7
28.	Kt — B 1 ch	K — R 8
29.	B — B 3 mate	

It will be seen that the ending is rather laborious.
There are two outstanding features: the close following by the King, and the controlling of the squares of
opposite colour to the Bishop by the combined action
of the Knight and King. The student would do well
to exercise himself methodically in this ending, as it
gives a very good idea of the actual power of the
pieces, and it requires foresight in order to accomplish
the mate within the fifty moves which are granted by
the rules.

7. QUEEN AGAINST ROOK

This is one of the most difficult endings without Pawns. The resources of the defence are many, and when used skilfully only a very good player will prevail within the limit of fifty moves allowed by the rules. (The rule is that at any moment you may demand that your opponent mate you within fifty moves. However, every time a piece is exchanged or a Pawn advanced the counting must begin afresh.)

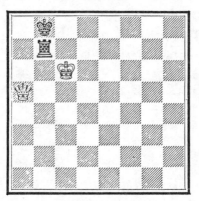

DIAGRAM 28
White to play

This is one of the standard positions which Black can often bring about. Now, it is White's move. If it were Black's move it would be simple, as he would have to move his Rook away from the King (find out why), and then the Rook would be comparatively easy to win. We deduce from the above that the main object is to force the Black Rook away from the defending King, and that, in order to compel Black

to do so, we must bring about the position in the
diagram with *Black* to move.   Once we know what is
required, the way to proceed becomes easier to find.
Thus:

> 1. Q — K 5 ch

Not 1 Q — R 6, because R — B 2 ch; 2 K — Kt 6,
R — B 3 ch; 3 K × R.   Stalemate.   (The beginner
will invariably fall into this trap.)

> 1. ....   K to R 1 or to R 2
> 2. Q — R 1 ch   K — Kt 1
> 3. Q — R 5

In a few moves we have accomplished our object.
The first part is concluded.   Now we come to the
second part.   The Rook can only go to a White
square, otherwise the first check with the Queen will
win it.   Therefore

> 3. ....   R — Kt 6
> 4. Q — K 5 ch   K — R 1 best
> 5. Q — R 8 ch   K — R 2
> 6. Q — Kt 7 ch   K — R 1
> 7. Q — Kt 8 ch   R — Kt 1
> 8. Q — R 2 mate

Now let us go back to Diagram 28 and suppose
that after 1 Q — K 5 ch, K — R 1 or K — R 2,
2 Q — R 1 ch, K — Kt 1, 3 Q — R 5 Black played
R — Kt 8 instead of R — Kt 6.   Then we have
4 Q — K 5 ch, K — R 2.

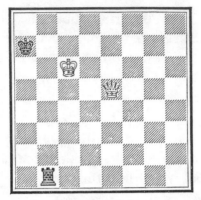

DIAGRAM 29
White to play

Now it will be all over in two moves, thus: 5 Q —
Q 4 ch, K — R 1; 6 Q — R 8 ch, and the R cannot
interpose because of Q — R 1 checkmate; and when
Black plays 6 . . . K — R 2, 7 Q — R 7 ch wins the R.

We have seen the main positions of this kind of
ending or rather the positions that must be finally
arrived at before obtaining a definite result; but to
drive the opposing pieces to such " Type Positions "
is at times extremely difficult. In fact there are some
positions where even most of the experts would fail
against a faultless defence, but it should always be
borne in mind that it is just as difficult to put up a
first-class defence as it is to make a first-class attack,
and that all other things being equal the player with
the better knowledge of these fundamentals and
" Type Positions " will have the better chance to succeed. It is outside the scope of this book to go into
such things as only the expert can handle. The object of the book is to put the reader in such a position

that he may by himself arrive at a point where he may be expert enough to tackle such problems. Besides, in actual practice, positions of that kind very rarely occur. Personally I do not remember to have ever had such positions when facing a first-class opponent.

We leave now the endings for the rest of the book.

8. THE MIDDLE GAME

Very little has been written on the subject. There is a book by Znosko-Borovsky called " The Middle Game in Chess." It is about the only book on the subject that I consider worth reading. Unfortunately the way the matter is approached in the book makes it difficult for the average player. Furthermore there is, in my opinion, a fundamental error at the very beginning of the book that makes more obscure the rest of the treatise.

At the very beginning of the book the author says: " The elements of chess are: —

1. Force, which is displayed in the Chessmen, or pieces, and acts in
2. Space, represented by the chess board, and
3. Time, developing with the moves."

From the above it should follow as the only logical conclusion, and chess is an essentially logical game, that if a player is ahead in all of the three elements he should have, at least, the better game. Yet as the author himself shows later, you may be ahead in all of the three elements and, nevertheless, have a completely lost game. Why? Because he has left out the element of *position*. It is true that later he speaks of valuation of the position, and of superior and inferior positions, but this does not correct the original statement. The fact is that chess consists of those three elements plus the inherent element of *position*, and that *position* is first, last, and foremost. Position, as the word indicates, has reference to the location of the pieces on the board; and it is generally valued by the greater or lesser mobility of the pieces, plus the pressure that these pieces may exert against different points of the chess-board, or against certain pieces of the opponent. In appraising the value of a given position the elements of Time, Space, and Force or Material should be considered. To the average player it will be simple to consider and appraise at its proper value the element of Force by simply taking the Pawn as a unit and applying the valuation of the pieces previously explained in the first part of this book.

The element of Space will be easy to value at times. At other times it will be rather difficult. And the element of Time will be far more elusive, with but few exceptions. In the end game the Time element is of more importance and also easier to value correctly.

Let us come back to the *middle game* and to the elements involved. It might be said that the thing for the reader to bear in mind is this: You may be behind in Force or Material and yet have a winning *position*. You may be behind in Time and yet have a winning *position*. You may be behind in Space and yet have a winning *position*. And finally you may be behind in all three of the other elements, Material, Space, and Time, and yet have a winning *position*.

This does not mean that you should neglect any of the other three elements, but that you should give pre-eminence to the element of *position*. Examples are given below illustrating each of the points mentioned above.

DIAGRAM 30
White to play

The position above is from a game between two players of average strength. It was arrived at as follows: 1 P — Q 4, P — Q 4; 2 P — Q B 4, P — K 3; 3 P — K 3, P — Q Kt 3; 4 Kt — K B 3, B — Q 3; 5 B — Q 3, P × P; 6 B × P, B — Kt 2; 7 Kt — B 3, Kt — K 2; 8 B — Q 3, O — O; 9 P — K 4, P — Q B 4. An analysis of the opening moves will show that Black has gained in time. Yet White can win the game now, as follows: 10 P — K 5, B — B 2; 11 B × P ch, K × B; 12 Kt — Kt 5 ch, K — Kt 3. (Best, since against K — Kt White would play Q — R 5.) 13 Q — Kt 4, Q × P. (Best. White threatened Kt × K P ch.) 14 B — B 4, P — B 4; 15 Q — Kt 3 and Black has no defence against White's multiple threats.

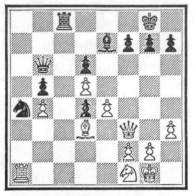

DIAGRAM 31
White to play

The above position is taken from a game Capa-
blanca-Dus-Chotimirsky played at St. Petersburg on
December 13, 1913. (See " My Chess Career " by
J. R. Capablanca.) Black has gained in space and
at first glance would seem to have the best of the
game. But White, through a series of very pretty
combinations, can win the game. The play continued
as follows:

P — K 5   25   P — Kt 3

To prevent White's threat of Q — B 5 and to block
the action of the B against the K R P.

P — K 6   26   R — B
Kt — Kt 3   27   Q — Kt 2

If P × P, Q — Kt 4, threatening both B × K Kt P,
and also Q × K P ch. Black probably wanted to
have his Q on the second line for the possible defence
of his K. (It is easy to see that by removing the B
Black's Q would be defending the whole K's side.)

Also he wanted to exchange Queens after P × P. The reader should notice the enormous force exerted by the entrance of the White Kt into the fray. This Kt will be the deciding factor.

Kt — B 5   28   P × P

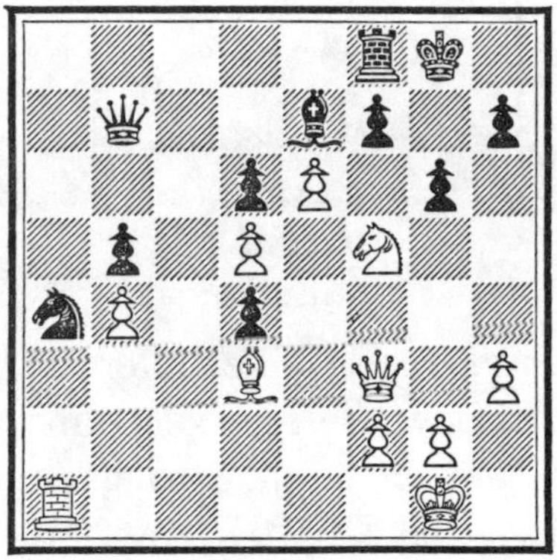

DIAGRAM 32
Black to play

K — R was best, but then Q — K 4 would have followed, with a sure win for White with proper play. Black had been wanting to take this P for some time, and had made his previous move with that intention. He did not want to wait any longer and thereby hastened the end. However, he had no valid defence in the position.

P × P   29   Q — B 2

Of course he could not take the Q because of Kt × B ch winning a piece.

Q — B 6   30

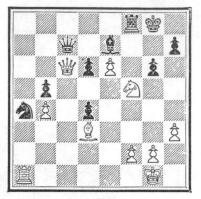

DIAGRAM 33
Black to play

The Q of course cannot be taken because of Kt ×
B ch. Notice how the Kt exerts an enormous pressure. (K B 5 is one of the strongest places for a Kt
when attacking the K castled on that side.) White's
Q's move accomplishes three things: it unpins the Kt,
it gains time by forcing the Black Q to move, and it
brings the Q in line with the White Bishop (after the
B takes the Q Kt P), controlling the diagonal Q R 4
— K 8. Later on, as a result of this manœuvre,
when the Queens are exchanged at Q 7, the White B
will remain there, controlling the square K 8, thus
protecting the advance of the passed K P of White
which will Queen at K 8. If the reader will carefully
consider all these moves and combinations he will
find not only the beauty of the whole thing but, what
is far more important for his progress, the under-
lying principle of the middle game: " Co-ordinating
the action of the pieces."

	30	Q — Q
Kt × B ch	31	Q × Kt

B × Q Kt P	32	Kt — B 6
Q — Q 7	33	Q × Q
B × Q	34	R — Q Kt

Black might just as well give up. Had he played Kt — Q 4, then 35 R — Q, R — B 5; 36 P — Kt 3, R — K 5; 37 B — B 6, R — K 4; 38 R × P, Kt — K 2; 39 R × P etc.

(35) P — K 7 and after some moves Black resigned.

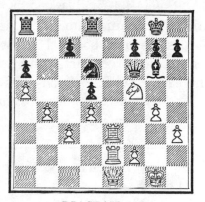

DIAGRAM 34
White to move

In the above diagram Black is ahead in " Force," and yet White wins easily as follows: 1 Kt × Kt, Q × Kt. (Black's best move was P — K R 4, but then with a Pawn more and a good *position* White should have no trouble winning the game.) 2 R — K 8 ch, R × R; 3 R × R ch, R × R; 4 Q × R ch, Q — B; 5 Q × Q ch, K × Q; 6 P — Kt 5 and Black cannot stop White from getting a Queen and thereby winning the game.

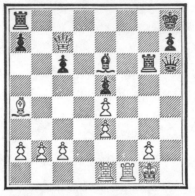

DIAGRAM 35   Black to move

The Position in the diagram above is taken from
Znosko-Borovsky's own book. Here White is ahead
in all three items, Force, Time, and Space; and yet
Black wins easily by R × P ch followed by R —
K Kt ch. The reason is simple: *position*.

DIAGRAM 36

Either White or Black to move

Again another position taken from Znosko's book.
Here again White is ahead in all three of the ele-

ments of Force, Time, and Space, and yet he cannot win the game simply because Black's *position* compensates these disadvantages.

The examples given should be sufficient for the reader to realize the true value of *position*. Let us now leave this matter for the time being and consider other points of importance with regard to the middle game.

9. CENTRE SQUARES

DIAGRAM 37

The squares K 4, Q 4, K 5 and Q 5 for both White and Black are the centre squares. They are the most valuable squares both in the opening and in the middle game, and often also in the end game. They deserve therefore special attention. A single glance will show that a B or a Q placed on any of these four squares will command more squares than anywhere else. Also a Kt placed on any of the four centre squares will be able to move over to either side faster than from any other place. Also in the end game the K placed on any of those four squares will be able to go faster to either side than from any other place. All this is simply a mathematical fact and in itself sufficient to show the importance of those squares. But there are other factors to show their importance. It has been stated already that the best first two opening moves, theoretically, are either P — Q 4 or P — K 4. That means that the four centre squares are the squares where the battle takes place immediately. Furthermore, as development takes place the pieces are brought out towards the centre of the board, thus perforce making the four centre squares of paramount importance. So far as the middle game is concerned, there is a general fundamental principle which says: " Control of the centre is an essential prerequisite to a successful direct attack against the King." By control of the centre is meant control of the four centre squares. Later it will be seen how this works in practice.

10. PAWN FORMATIONS

DIAGRAM 38

Best central Pawn formation in early stages

Very seldom will an expert permit his opponent to hold such a central formation of Pawns for any length of time. He will quickly challenge it by advancing his own centre Pawns or either of the B Pawns in order to break it up thus:

DIAGRAM 39
Pawn position from a French Defence

The formation of White's centre Pawns is immediately challenged.

DIAGRAM 40
Pawn position from a Sicilian Defence

The Q P is not permitted to come up level with the K P without the possibility of being captured.

DIAGRAM 41

Pawn position from a Ruy Lopez, Giuoco Piano.
Four Knights, three Knights and other openings

Again the same as in the previous case.

DIAGRAM 42

Pawn position from a Dutch Defence

The K P is not permitted to come up level with the Q P.

DIAGRAM 43

Pawn position from Q. P. openings

The K P is not permitted to come up level with the Q P.

We have seen now what takes place in all of the leading openings, according to the best expert opinion. No better proof is needed of the importance of the four centre squares and of the centre Pawn formation.

II. CASTLED PAWN FORMATION

DIAGRAM 44

Best defensive " castled Pawn position " against frontal attack

It has already been stated that castling on the K's side is generally safer. In all the following illustrations it is assumed that castling has taken place on the K's side. The above position is the best defensive Pawn position against frontal attacks. The one thing to guard against in such a position is a possible check by either R or Q on the first rank. Since during the middle game such danger very seldom exists, it is advisable after castling to hold such a formation of Pawns until circumstances force you to change it.

DIAGRAM 45
Excellent castled Pawn formation

An excellent position. Not so strong defensively against a frontal attack as the previous position, but nearly as good, and it provides an outlet for the King against a check on the first rank. In practice, in most games, this will be found to be an excellent Pawn position. There are some good reasons why the previous position is better than this one, but such reasons only experience can demonstrate. Against an average player the position of Diagram 45 will prove just as good as that of Diagram 44, if not better. It is only when facing an expert that the thing may change.

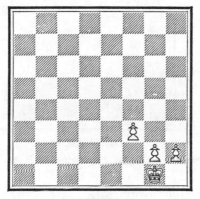

DIAGRAM 46
Deficient castled Pawn formation

Not so good, but not yet bad. The disadvantage of this position is that it exposes the King to check along the diagonal and that in order to avoid it White would have to play K — R, thus losing time. Furthermore the K at R sq would be in the worst possible position for an ending of K and Pawns, since the K would be farthest away from the centre of the board and from the Q's side Pawns.

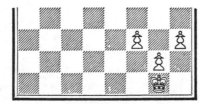

DIAGRAM 47
Bad Pawn formation (V Pawn formation)

DIAGRAM 48
Bad Pawn formation (Inverted V Pawn formation)

Bad defensive formations. Besides, the V and inverted V formation of Pawns create so-called " holes," or places between the Pawns where an enemy piece may be posted. A piece posted in such " holes " can be attacked only by another piece.

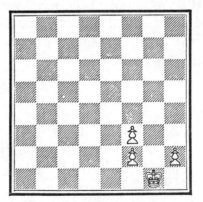

DIAGRAM 49
Very bad Pawn formation

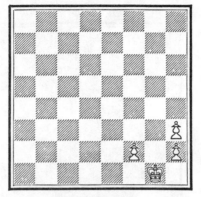

DIAGRAM 50
Very bad Pawn formation

Very bad Pawn formation. The Pawns are broken
up and can only be defended by pieces. Furthermore
the King is wide open to all kinds of attacks.

12. TYPE POSITIONS AND COMBINATIONS

It is now time for the reader to familiarize himself
with a number of " Type " positions and combinations that are apt to present themselves during the
middle game.

Let us consider the position of Diagram 51. It is
from a game Lasker-Bauer at Amsterdam in 1889.
The forces are even. All White would have to do
would be to play Q × Kt. The centre Pawn formation is in favour of White, since he controls three out
of the four centre squares. Furthermore the two
White Bishops are in an ideal attacking position, the
best attacking position in fact, for two Bishops against
a King castled on the K's side. If White plays the
natural move Q × Kt, Black will answer with

Black: Bauer

White: Dr. E. Lasker
DIAGRAM 51
White to move

P — K B 4 blocking the action of the B at Q 3, and will follow that move with B — B 3 blocking the action of the B at Kt 2. White would in any case have a satisfactory game, but he wants to gain something, if he can, from the advantageous position of his Bishop, and his command of the centre. From those factors he now evolves a very pretty combination, winning the game in a few moves thus: — 1 B × P ch, K × B; 2 Q × Kt ch, K — Kt; 3 B × P, K × B; 4 Q — Kt 4 ch, K — R 2; 5 R — B 3, P — K 4; 6 R — R 3 ch, Q — R 3; 7 R × Q ch, K × R; 8 Q — Q 7 and White has an easily won game. This " Type " of combination does not occur very frequently, yet it is well to remember it. Such a well-known master as Nimzovitsch was caught by Dr. Tarrasch, at St. Petersburg in 1914, in a similar position.

Black: Dr. S. Tarrasch

White: A. Nimzovitsch

DIAGRAM 52

White to play. From a game Nimzovitsch-Tarrasch at the St. Petersburg International Masters Tournament, 1914

Black's last move was P from Q 4 to Q 5 uncovering the B at B 3. Notice the position of the two Bishops: " the strongest attacking position for the two Bs against a K castled on the K's side." White played P × P, whereupon followed B × P ch, K × B, Q — R 5 ch, K — Kt, B × P and Black won in a few moves. In this position White played P — B 3. Had he played K × B then Q — Kt 5 ch, followed by R — Q 3 and mate at R 3. Compare this example with the previous one and see how exactly alike are both combinations. This should be ample proof to the reader of the value of such " Type " positions and " Type " combinations. It is evident that in similar positions to those shown above there will be similar combinations to those of the text.

There are other " Types " of positions which are apt to occur more frequently. Take for instance:

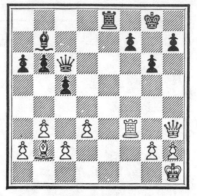

DIAGRAM 53
White to move

Black threatens mate, and if White had to defend it, Black would get an excellent game. White, however, mates in three moves as follows: 1 Q × P ch, K × Q. 2 R — R 3 ch, K — Kt. 3 R — R 8 ch mate.

This same type of combination may come as the result of a somewhat more complicated position.

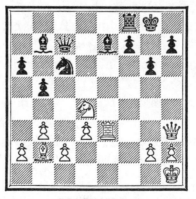

DIAGRAM 54

White is a piece behind, and unless he can win it back quickly he will lose; he therefore plays:

1. Kt × Kt   B — Kt 4

He cannot take the Kt because White threatens mate
by Q × P ch followed by R — R 3 ch.

2. Kt — K 7 ch   Q × Kt

Again if B × Kt; Q × P ch, K × Q; R — R 3 ch,
King moves; R — R 8 mate.

3. R × Q   B × R
4. Q — Q 7

and White wins one of the two Bishops, remains
with a Q and a B against a R and B, and should
therefore win easily. These two examples show the
danger of advancing the K Kt P one square, after
having castled on that side.

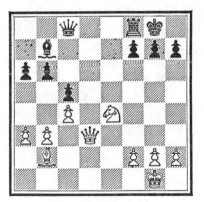

DIAGRAM 55

This is another very interesting type of combination. Black has a R for a Kt and should therefore
win, unless White is able to obtain some compensation immediately. White, in fact, mates in a few
moves thus: 1. Kt — B 6 ch   P × Kt

Forced, otherwise Q × P mates.

> 2. Q — Kt 3 ch   K — R 1
> 3. B × P mate.

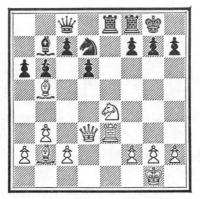

DIAGRAM 56

The same type of combination occurs in a more complicated form in the above position.

> 1. B × Kt   Q × B

If...B × Kt; Q — B 3 threatens mate, and therefore wins the Q, which is already attacked.

> 2. Kt — B 6 ch   P × Kt
> 3. R — Kt 3 ch   K — R 1
> 4. B × P mate.

A very frequent type of combination is shown in Diagram 57.

Here White is the exchange and a Pawn behind, but he can win quickly thus: 1 B × P ch, K × B. (If 1...K — R 1; 2 Q — K R 5, P — K Kt 3; 3 Q — R 6, and wins.)

DIAGRAM 57

2 Q — R 5 ch, K — Kt 1; 3 Kt — Kt 5, and Black cannot stop mate at K R 7 except by sacrificing the Queen by Q — K 5, which would leave White with a Q for a R.

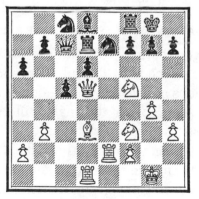

DIAGRAM 58

This same type of combination is seen in a more complicated form in the position above.

White proceeds as follows: 1 Kt × Kt ch (this clears the line for the B); B × Kt (to stop the Kt from moving to Kt 5 after the sacrifice of the B);

2 R × B, Kt × R best; 3 B × P ch, K × B. (If
3...K — R 1; 4 Q — R 5, P — K Kt 3; 5 B × P ch,
K — Kt 2; 6 Q — R 7 ch, K — B 3; 7 P — Kt 5 ch,
K — K 3; 8 B × P ch, R × B; 9 Q — K 4 mate.)
4 Q — R 5 ch, K — Kt 1; 5 Kt — Kt 5, R — B 1;
6 Q — R 7 ch, K — B 1; 7 Q — R 8 ch, Kt — Kt 1;
8 Kt — R 7 ch, K — K 2; 9 R — K 1 ch, K — Q 1;
10 Q × Kt mate.

This combination is rather long and has many variations, therefore a beginner will hardly be able to
fathom it; but, knowing the type of combination,
he might under similar circumstances undertake and
carry out a brilliant attack which he would otherwise
never think of. It will be seen that all the combinations shown have for a foundation the proper co-ordination of the pieces, which have all been brought to
bear against a weak point.

13. VALUATION OF POSITION IN THE MIDDLE GAME

To judge accurately the value of an involved position is one of the most difficult things in chess. Certain positions are easy to judge, others are extremely
difficult. Very often the main difference between
two experts is the superior ability of one over the
other in judging accurately the value of the different
positions during the course of a game. From his con-
clusions regarding any given position the chess master
decides on the procedure to follow. It is evident that
a profound discussion of this aspect of the game
would be beyond the scope of this book. Certain
general lines, however, may be given that will help
the average player to decide which side has the better

position. The first thing to look at is material. If one side is one Pawn ahead that constitutes an advantage, and very often a decisive advantage among players of equal strength. To upset such an advantage there must be for the other player a much greater freedom of action for his pieces (that would generally be gain in Space), or he would need to have the possibility of a strong attack against some weak point which would result in his recovering at least the Pawn lost. As a compensation he might also have an attack against the King involving the possibility of mate. This latter alternative would be much more common among average players, as they are generally more apt to see a chance for an attack against the King than for an attack against weak points.

The second thing to consider would be the greater or lesser freedom of the pieces together with the greater or lesser chances of co-ordinating their action. A cramped position is a bad position. An open position with freedom for the pieces, but with the pieces so placed that their action cannot be co-ordinated for some time, is a bad position. In general the things to consider are: — Force, Freedom of manœuvre, and Co-ordination of the action of the pieces. Let us look at some examples from actual play.

In Diagram 59 White is a Pawn ahead. The K's side Pawns of both sides are united and in good formation. Black's Q's side Pawns are isolated and cannot advance. White's lonesome P on the Q's side is very much in the same situation. The Black

Black: M. Vidmar

White: A. Rubinstein
DIAGRAM 59
White to play.　From a game Rubinstein-Vidmar,
International Masters Tournament, London, 1922

B at Q 4 is in a commanding position, better posted
than White's B, and the Black Q is ready to co-
operate with the B in a possible attack against White's
King.　But a Q and B alone are not enough for such
an attack against a solid defensive position such as
White has on his K's side.　It does not take much time
to arrive at the conclusion that White has a winning
position.　In the actual game White played P — K 4.
(The P cannot be taken because of P — Kt 3 winning
the B.)　This was done in order to drive away the B
from the commanding position at Q 4.　It was a very
energetic way to continue the game, but if White did
not have such a move at his disposal he could play
R — Q B attacking the B P and making room for his
B at K B 1, in case it should be found convenient to
bring it back to the defence of his K.　In fact, even
if it were Black's move and he made his strongest
threat Q — Kt 4, White could answer with either

P — B 3 or P — Kt 3 and still have a winning game because of the great preponderance of Pawns on the K's side.

Black: M. Euwe

White: E. Znosko-Borovsky

DIAGRAM 60

Black to play. From a game Znosko-Borovsky — Euwe, International Masters Tournament, London, 1922

Again one of the players, Black in this case, is a Pawn ahead, and he has a solid Pawn formation. He may have trouble from the fact that one of his Kts is pinned by the White B. White has a broken Pawn formation and if it comes to an ending he must lose. His only chance is to attack the Black King. White threatens to play Kt — K 4 followed by either B × Kt or Kt × Kt and then R — K Kt, etc. All this is possible because the B is pinning the Black Kt and because of the greater power of the B over the Kt in an open board. Yet so large is the advantage of Black in material, because of the extra P combined with the broken Pawn formation of White, that I am inclined to believe Black would have a very good game even if it were White's move. This belief is based on the fact that if it were White's move and White played Kt — K 4, Black could reply Kt × Kt and obtain an excellent game.

However, as it is Black's move he can avoid all trouble by attacking at once, thus taking the initiative away from his opponent. His best move is Kt — Q 5, threatening both Kt × Q B P and Kt — B 4, and also making room for his Q at Q B 3. White would not be able to parry all these threats. In the actual game Black made a very bad move: 23 R — K. The game continued: 24 R — K Kt. (White threatens many things now, among them a very pretty combination beginning with R × P ch.) The position is most interesting. Black made another bad move 24...Kt — K 2 and lost because of 25 Q R — Q, Q — B 3; 26 B × Kt, Q × B; 27 Kt — K 4, Q — B 3; 28 Kt — Q 6 winning the exchange. The fact is that Black had only one satisfactory move, a very difficult move to find, and yet a very logical move; that move was 24...Kt — K R 4. Then might follow: 25 Kt — K 4, Q — K 3; 26 Q — Kt 5, P — B 4. (The saving move; Black gives back the extra Pawn but is now able to co-ordinate the action of his pieces for the defence of his King, and then because of the superiority of his Pawn formation should be able to obtain a winning game. The position after Black's initial error, R — K, is full of possibilities and will repay a close study.

Black: D. Janowski

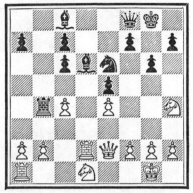

White: J. R. Capablanca

DIAGRAM 61

White to play. From a game Capablanca-Ja-
nowski, Havana International Tournament, 1913

White is the " Exchange " or " Quality " ahead.
His Pawn formation is good and there are no immediate mate-threatening attacks by Black; therefore
White with proper play should win the game. In the
actual game White did not adopt the best defensive
course, and consequently had trouble; but nevertheless because of his material advantage he was finally
able to win.

The position of Diagram 62 is very difficult to judge
accurately. Black has three Pawns for a Kt, and apparently a very strong attack against White's King.
In material White is actually a little ahead. During
the opening and early middle game a Kt or B is worth
more than three Pawns. If the three Pawns were on
the Q's side where they could be advanced quickly,
then Black would be better off in material. But the
three Pawns are on the K's side and cannot be freely

Black: F. D. Yates

White: R. Reti

DIAGRAM 62

White to play. London International Tournament, 1922

advanced because they are needed for the protection
of the King. If Black had no attack there would not
be any question about White having the best of the
game, but there is an attack, and that factor must be
considered in appraising the value of the position.
If the attack can be beaten off without suffering
any additional loss either in Time, Space, or Material, the position of White must perforce be improved, and in that case it would be White for
choice. In this position almost every expert would
take Black for choice. The average player should
take Black for choice. In such positions the defence
is far more difficult than the attack. Besides, the
average player should always try to play an attacking
game, and when such an opportunity presents itself
he should not hesitate. My personal opinion is that
by playing R — Q 2, White could stand off all of
Black's threats, and if that is the case it would be

White for choice. In the actual game White played Q — Q 7, a bad move which would have lost had Black countered with R — (B 4) — B 2, driving the Q away from the diagonal K R 3 — Q B 8, and followed with R — B 3 threatening R — K Kt 3. Black, however, failed to make the right move and lost.

It is not the purpose of this chapter to play out these positions, but merely to consider them in a general way in order to ascertain the true value of the position. Let us go back to the position on the diagram and study it further. Black's immediate threat is R — R 4 to be followed by Q — R 6 and mate at R 8. White's move Q — Q 7 was made to prevent such a thing, but it was wrong because the Q could be driven off and another threat made that could not be stopped. The move that I propose, R — Q 2, stops all those threats. It makes room for the B at Q 1, where it would attack the Q at B 6 and at the same time control the diagonal Q 1 — K R 5. The move R — Q 2 also keeps latent the threat of Q — Q 7, which this time would be very effective if permitted to materialize. The move R — Q 2 also liberates the B at K 3 which now cannot be moved because of P — K 6, threatening Q × Kt mate. But after R — Q 2, P — K 6 would be met by P × P, the R at Q 2 defending the Kt at Kt 2. Once the B at K 3 can be moved to some place, for instance K B 4, there would be room for the Kt at Kt 2 to go to K 3, and thus slowly the White pieces would be worked into better positions. At the same time White's position would become freer. And if all this could be accomplished without loss of Material, Space, or Time, then there should not be any doubt as to which side had the better of it.

Black: E. Znosko-Borovsky

White: J. R. Capablanca
DIAGRAM 63
White to play. London International Tournament, 1922

This is a different type of position. In this case it is easy to see who has the advantage. White's position is solid, with no weakness, good Pawn formation and good co-ordination of the pieces. Black on the other side has some holes in his position: his pieces cannot work all together; the Pawn formation is bad on both sides, especially on the Q's side, and the Black squares on the Q's side are fully controlled by White. From the above it is evident that White must have a won position, since Black has no compensation for his many weak points. In the game White won as follows: 23 Kt — B 5, B — B; 24 Kt × R P, B — Kt 2; 25 Kt — B 5, B — B; 26 Kt (B 5) — Q 3,

B — Kt 2; 27 R — B 2, R — B; 28 K R — Q B, K R — K; 29 P — Q R 4 and White won easily. This example is interesting only because it shows the weaknesses of such position as Black had.

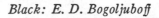
Black: E. D. Bogoljuboff

White: J. R. Capablanca
DIAGRAM 64
White to move.   London International Tournament, 1922

This is a difficult position to judge.   The Pawn formation is bad both for White and for Black, but Black has an advanced passed Q R P which threatens to go on to Q.   Black's Q, R, and Kt are placed offensively and have more freedom than White's pieces. White on the other hand has all his pieces placed defensively and both his K P and Q B P are subjected to attack.   The only way to defend them both would be to play Kt — Q 2, but then Black would answer with Q — Kt 5 and the Q R P of Black would be free to advance.   On these counts it is all in Black's favour, and if there were no other important considerations

it would be all over with White. There is, however, a
very important item in White's favour and that is the
position of Black's B at K R 2. That B is not only
cut off completely from the action of the game but,
what is worse, it has no way to come into play. White
is therefore playing as though he were a piece ahead.
On that assumption, White must take the initiative,
if at all possible, in order to make his extra force tilt
the balance in his favour. Actually the game continued: 36 Kt — Q 4, Q × Q (Black could not play
Q × P because of R — B 2 followed by Kt — K 6,
leaving him in a helpless situation); 37 R × Q,
R — Kt; 38 R — Q B 3, K — B 2; 39 K — B 3,
R — Kt 7; 40 Kt (Kt 3) — K 2.

Black: E. D. Bogoljuboff

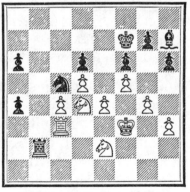

White: J. R. Capablanca
DIAGRAM 65
Black to move

There cannot be any question now as to which side
has the better game. Black's Bishop is still out of the
game while the White Knights are getting together

preparatory to the final assault. In the actual game Black resigned on his 52nd move. This example shows how valuable is the knowledge of the Fundamental Principles, and how well rewarded their application.

Black: G. Maroczy

White: Z. Borovsky

DIAGRAM 66

White to play. London International Tournament, 1922

The valuation here is rather simple. Black's single P at Q R 5 holds the two of White on the Q's side while Black's extra P on the K's side is free and can be stopped from advancing only by one of White's pieces. Black furthermore has two Bishops. For the rest the positions are very much the same, and therefore Black must have the best of the game. Actually the game was drawn, but several errors were made on both sides.

Black: V. Wahltuch

White: E. D. Bogoljuboff

DIAGRAM 67

White to move. London International Tournament, 1922

Here again valuation is simple. The forces are
equal, but Black has three weak Pawns — the K P,
Q B P, and Q R P. The Q R P would be strong and a
source of worry to White if it were far advanced and
properly protected, but in its backward position it
can only be a weakness. Black's one good point is
the possession of an open file by one of his Rooks.
If the B at K 1 could be placed at Q 4 via Q B 3, thus
protecting one of the weak Pawns and at the same
time exerting pressure along the long diagonal,
Black's game would not be bad; but such is not the
case, because White's first move will be B — R 4.
White on his side has no weak point at all. His
wedge-like formation of Pawns is very strong ag-
gressively. He also has enough freedom of manœuvre for his pieces. From the above it is evident
that the advantage must rest with White. White's
first move in this position was B — R 4 in order to

exchange the B, thus stopping it from going to Q 4 and also taking away a possible defender of the weak Q B P and the weak K P. The move also frees the Q, which now may enter Black's territory via Q R 2.

In the actual game White very soon won a couple of Pawns, the weak Q B P and K P, and shortly afterward Black resigned. The different examples shown should give the reader a good idea of the way to judge the value of a given position. We now leave this part of the game to go into the chapter on the openings.

14. THE OPENINGS

Probably the books on the openings outnumber all the other chess books put together. Almost all of these books are purely technical and therefore of very little value to the average player. There are thousands of variations in a single opening. Take the Ruy Lopez for instance; it would be easy to write a whole book on this opening alone. Such a book would be very valuable to the expert, but of very little use to the average player. The expert, with his thorough knowledge of the game, would derive great benefit from a book which would exhaust or nearly exhaust the possibilities of a single opening. The expert could go through such a book in a very short time and master everything in it. The average player could not do such a thing. Besides, after going through the opening stages, the expert would know how to handle the middle game and the end game in such a way as to derive all possible advantage from his knowledge of the opening. The average player cannot do this. For him the study of such a book requires a great deal of patience and time, more than most people are willing to devote to the study of the game of chess. A book of this type is a dry book, and all things considered does not pay, except as a sort of encyclopedia or reference book. Being purely technical, such books do not teach the general laws and principles which govern a game of chess.

It is for these reasons that I have always considered purely technical books on the openings as fit only for experts or near experts. For the average player it is better to have a book dealing with the openings in a more general way. To the expert every little detail counts, but the average player cannot concern himself with such minute analysis, and must limit himself to broad lines of a general character, with the assurance that if the principles are sound he is bound to come out in good shape. Method and care are needed in the opening. The whole structure of the game may be the result of the first few moves. For the sake of experience and practice it may be well to vary the openings, but for the sake of efficiency it might be better to stick to one single opening for the attack, and one single opening or method of development for the defence. This system may be followed until the one opening in question has been mastered. Then the player may take up a new opening, and thus gradually reach the point where he feels familiar with half a dozen different openings. Half a dozen different openings, well learned, are about all the average player needs to obtain good results. Later on, if he finds it convenient and to his liking, he may try still others. He should consider the opening simply as that early part of the game, where his object should be to bring out his pieces with method and care in order to build a solid *Position* from which later he will be able to evolve his plans and combinations for the middle game.

Let us now see the practical application of the ideas expounded above.

DIAGRAM 68

There is a double problem confronting the player before the first move is made: to bring his pieces into action as quickly as possible, but to do so in such a way as to control as much as possible the four centre squares. If White could evolve a plan whereby he might within a few moves get his pieces out and at the same time obtain undoubted control of the centre, White would theoretically have a winning *Position*. It therefore follows that White should strive for such a thing while Black must try to block the attempt. White, having the first move, has the initiative. The initiative means time and action, and is therefore an advantage. With these facts in mind it is easier to see what is to be done. There are four Pawn moves, namely P — K B 4, P — K 4, P — Q 4, and P — Q B 4, which would immediately begin the attempt to control the centre. Of these four moves P — K B 4 is the only one which does not open the way for the action of one of the pieces and should therefore be the weakest of the four moves. Next in line comes P — Q B 4 which opens the way for the Q only. And finally there are the other two moves, P — K 4 and P — Q 4, which open the way for the Q and a B, and should therefore be the two best opening moves. There are yet two other opening moves, Kt — K B 3 and Kt — Q B 3, which would seem to fill the bill. They are both good moves, especially Kt — K B 3, but for the purpose of this book it is better not to take them up to the present time. It might indeed be well to state at once that White can make almost any move for a first move without getting a bad game. The only exceptions would be P — K Kt 4, P — K B 3 and possibly Kt — K R 3 and Kt — Q R 3. P — K R 4 would be a poor opening move, and to a lesser extent P — Q R 4. Black's choice, on the other hand, is far more restricted, and against certain moves of White the choice is very limited indeed. Let us now go back to Diagram 68 and examine one of White's two best opening moves:

White		Black
P — K 4	1	

Black has the choice of four moves recognized as the best answers to White's opening move. These four moves are P — K 4 (probably the best), P — K 3 (the so-called French defence), P — Q B 3 (the Caro-Kann defence), and P — Q B 4 (the Sicilian defence). By choosing one of the last three moves and playing it all the time, a player will soon become familiar with this type of game and probably obtain good results. He will however lose a great deal of the fun of the game through lack of variety. He will also work less with his imagination and not be so keen when faced with a new problem. According to his own temperament and inclination, the player should decide whether to use regularly one single opening or play any of several openings.

1   P — K 4

It is now White who has the choice. He may play 2 Kt — K B 3 (the best move) or Kt — Q B 3 or B — B 4, all standard moves, and he could also play a centre gambit by P — Q 4 or a King's gambit by P — K B 4. The gambit moves on the King's side are inferior. They have for object to draw away Black's centre Pawn in order to obtain a better control of the centre. Experience has shown, however, that in either case Black may safely take the Pawn and quickly equalize the game or get the better of it. Formerly, before the study of the game had advanced as in late years, the masters indulged in all kinds of gambits. Nowadays, with one or two exceptions, no good player would use such gambits in a serious contest. Later on we will give the main variations of these gambits to show why they are not played by the experts.

Kt — K B 3   2   Kt — Q B 3

Black could have also played either Kt — K B 3, the Petroff or Russian defence, or P — Q 3, the Philidor defence. Both those moves are considered by the majority of the experts as slightly inferior to the text move. Any other move would be vastly inferior. Thus B — B 4 is bad because of Kt × P, White winning a Pawn without sufficient compensation for Black. 2...P — K B 3 would be fatal because of Kt × P threatening check at R 5, and 2... Q — B 3 would not be good because of either Kt — Q B 3 or P — Q 4 giving White a great advantage in development. In general it is bad play to bring the Q out so early in the game, before a couple of minor pieces are out. The Q needs the help of the minor pieces either for protection or for attack.

B — Kt 5   3

Probably the best move in this position. This constitutes the Ruy Lopez, one of the oldest and best of the openings. With the exception of the Q's Gambit, it is probably the strongest opening for White. So far every move of White has been both of a developing and of an attacking nature.

3   P — Q 3

The original Steinitz defence. A purely defensive move which by itself justifies White's choice of moves. There are other defences such as 3 P — Q R 3 followed, after 4 B — R 4, by either 4 Kt — B 3 or 4 P — Q 3. It is also followed by 4 B — B 4, but I consider that move inferior to the other two. Personally I favour, now, the defence 3...P — Q R 3;

4 B — R 4, P — Q 3.   I believe it gives Black a
better chance to make a counter demonstration and
assume the initiative at the slightest error on White's
part.   Other defences, such as 3...K Kt — K 2 or
B — B 4 or Q — B 3, are vastly inferior, as would be
also 3...B.— K 2 which would be met by P — Q 4.
3...K Kt — K 2 would be met by P — Q 4.   3...
Q — B 3 would be met by Kt — B 3, and 3...B —
B 4 would be met by P — Q B 3 followed by P — Q 4.
Careful consideration will show how quickly White
would gain in development after any weak defensive
move by Black.   That is the point for the student to
bear in mind.

P — Q 4	4	B — Q 2

Black does not want to give up the centre and therefore defends his K P indirectly.   The student should
thoroughly analyse these situations.   In this variation
all of White's opening moves are very forceful, while
Black's parries are full of finesse.

Kt — B 3	5	Kt — B 3
O — O	6	B — K 2
R — K	7	

White's last move is Dr. Tarrasch's combination to
force Black to exchange his centre Pawn and give up
the centre.   It is a deep-laid trap.   Apparently
nothing has been changed by the last move, and yet
if Black should now castle, he will either lose a Pawn
or the quality.   Thus: 7...O — O; 8 B × Kt,
B × B; 9 P × P, P × P; 10 Q × Q, Q R × Q;
11 Kt × P, B × P; 12 Kt × B, Kt × Kt; 13

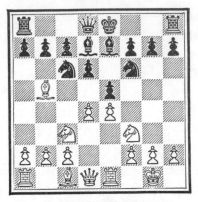

DIAGRAM 69

Black to play. Position after White's 7th move

Kt — Q 3, P — K B 4; 14 P — K B 3, B — B 4 ch; 15 Kt × B, Kt × Kt; 16 B — Kt 5, R — Q 4; 17 B — K 7, R — K; 18 P — Q B 4 and Black must either lose the Kt or give up the R for the B. Since Black needs to castle in order to continue his development, he must play as follows:

	8	P × P
Kt × P	9	O — O

White has gained the control of the centre, but Black's position is very solid. Experience has shown that a good defensive player can hold his own in such a position. Many games have continued: 10 B × Kt, P × B; 11 B — Kt 5, R — K; 12 Q — Q 3, P — K R 3; 13 B — R 4, Kt — R 2; 14 B × B, R × B. The position is worth study. White has no apparent weak point, and has freedom for his pieces, but he has nothing to attack. Black's position is solid and the B at Q 2 becomes a tower of strength. At times, Black

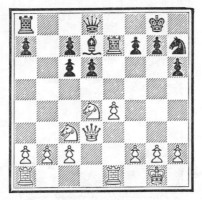

DIAGRAM 70

White to move. Position after Black's 14th move

in this position has played his Q to Q Kt, attacking White's Q Kt P, and then brought it forward to Q Kt 3, defending the whole Q's side and making room for his Q R which will go to K sq. The Kt at R 2 is worked around *via* K B and K 3, or *via* K Kt 4 and K 3, to exchange one of the White Kts, or to go either to Q B 4 or K B 5. At other times it is worked *via* K B to K Kt 3 where it is kept in reserve to go to K 4 or K B 5 as the occasion demands. If the Queens are exchanged Black has a good ending because of the superiority of the B over the Kt in endings with Pawns on both sides of the board, and also because the combination of R and B is generally stronger than the combination of R and Kt. Black's only real weakness is his isolated Q R P, but it is evident that it will be rather difficult to attack this P. Because this position has not been found so satisfactory for White as it appears at first glance, the experts have tried to improve White's play after move 6.

DIAGRAM 71

White to play.   Position after Black's 6th move

Instead of playing now R — K to force P × P, some have tried 7 B × Kt, B × B; 8 Q — Q 3, threatening to win a Pawn and forcing 8...P × P; 9 Kt × P, B — Q 2 (the B is too valuable to allow the exchange at Q B 3); 10 B — K Kt 5 with a very solid position and a freer game than Black.   Black on the other hand has a solid position and no weak isolated Pawn, but he has much less freedom of movement than before.   Yet it cannot be said that White has a winning position.   Good defensive play will probably get Black out of trouble.

We have now gone over one of the main variations of this most important opening.   Because of its importance we are giving below some of the main variations used by the experts, with very light comments of a general nature.

RUY LOPEZ

White		Black
P — K 4	1	P — K 4
Kt — K B 3	2	Kt — Q B 3
B — Kt 5	3	P — Q R 3
B — R 4	4	P — Q 3

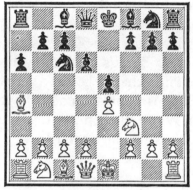

DIAGRAM 72

White to move.   Position after Black's 4th move
P — Q 3

Black's third move P — Q R 3 constitutes the so-called Morphy defence, since that great player always made this move against the Ruy Lopez. By combining this move with P — Q 3, the Steinitz defence, we have what might very well be called a Morphy-Steinitz defence. Why it has not been called that is hard to say. It would link two of the greatest names in all the history of Chess. The advantage of this combination of moves are mainly twofold: it threatens P — B 4, which would be a threat to White's centre and also a threat to take the initiative away from White; and it also prevents White from playing

P — Q 4 at once because of 5...P — Q Kt 4; 6 B — Kt 3, Kt × P; 7 Kt × Kt, P × Kt; and White cannot play 8 Q × P because of 8...P — Q B 4 followed by P — Q B 5, winning a piece. White would therefore have to continue with 8 B — Q 5, R — Kt; 9 Q × P, Kt — B 3, and Black has a very good game because of the time gained in developing his pieces.

Let us go back to the position in the diagram. White may play 5 B × Kt ch, P × B; 6 P — Q 4. Black may now play P — K B 3, holding the centre. It is true that Black's position will be somewhat cramped, but in exchange he has a very compact game with two Bishops, always an advantage; and the absence of a White Bishop on the White diagonals makes Black's King much safer.

White		Black
First 3 moves the same as before		
B × Kt	4	Q P × B
P — Q 4	5	P × P
Q × P	6	Q × Q
Kt × Q	7	B — Q 3

White has four Pawns to three on the K's side, while Black's double Pawn on the Q's side makes his preponderance of Pawns on that side of less consequence. If all the pieces were taken away from the board at this moment, White would have a winning K and P ending. It is on that assumption that White plays this variation. It follows that it is to White's advantage to exchange from now on. Black on the

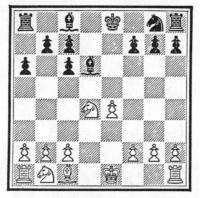

DIAGRAM 73

White to play. Position after Black's 7th move

other hand has two Bishops and a very free game, and should derive some benefit from it. It is my personal opinion that the Black King in this variation should be kept on the K's side, so that as pieces are exchanged and fewer are left on the board the Black King may be ready to meet the advance of White's Pawns on the K's side where White has the preponderance of force. In Pawn endings, whenever possible, the King must become a fighting piece.

White		Black
First 3 moves the same as before		
B — R 4	4	Kt — B 3
O — O	5	B — K 2
R — K	6	P — Q Kt 4
B — Kt 3	7	P — Q 3
P — B 3	8	O — O
P — Q 4	9	P × P

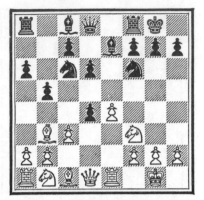

DIAGRAM 74

White to play.   Position after Black's 9th move

This move in conjunction with the previous one is Bogoljuboff's idea.   He disrupts the balance or equilibrium of the position.   Apparently he gives up the centre, but that is only for a moment.   As soon as White plays 10 P × P, he plays 10...B — Kt 5, threatening B × Kt, and if White answers with 11 B — K 3 he continues with 11...Kt — Q R 4 threatening to exchange one of the Bishops and ready to play P — Q B 4 when convenient, breaking up White's centre and obtaining a preponderance of Pawns on the Q's side against White's preponderance of Pawns on the K's side.   Since the Black Pawns are not only advanced but are free to continue their advance, while the White Pawns on the K's side are handicapped by the presence of the K behind them, the resulting position from that point of view would be all in Black's favour.   White, however, has compensation elsewhere.   Besides White can stop the whole scheme by playing on his 11 move Kt —

B 3 instead of B — K 3. Should Black then play
11...B × Kt, 12 P × B would give White an excellent game. All these variations should prove to the
student that if the development is made along sound
lines there will always be a way to meet any scheme
that the adversary may try to concoct.

White   Black

First 7 moves the same as before

White		Black
P — B 3	8	Kt — Q R 4
B — B 2	9	P — B 4
P — Q 4	10	Q — B 2

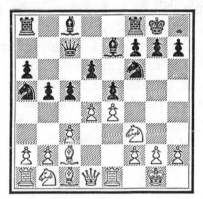

DIAGRAM 75

White to move. Position after Black's 10th move

A very old form of defence. As usual, development
has taken place in a battle for the control of the
centre. Both positions are solid, but Black has a
weaker Pawn formation. Black generally plays back
his Kt to B 3 in order to induce White to declare his
intentions in the centre. Should White play P × P,
Black would be rid of his backward Q P, and the B

at K 2 would be a little freer to move. White will of course avoid the exchange unless he obtains compensation elsewhere. White generally keeps his centre Pawns where they are now as long as he can, meanwhile working his Q Kt around *via* Q 2 and K B 1 to K 3, to post it later at Q 5, the hole in Black's position. Or he may advance his P to Q 5 to block the Q's side after he has worked his Q Kt around to K B 1 *via* Q 2. Then he will play P — K R 3 and P — K Kt 4 followed by Kt — Kt 3, and thus start an attack against Black's King. From the above it is evident that as usual White has the initiative. Black's role will be to prevent White from carrying out these schemes, or to be ready to meet the onslaught. Black's chances, as in all similar positions, will be to take the initiative at the first opportunity, and through the advance on the Q's wing to obtain the decision. Black's Q's side Pawns, according to the theories expounded in the text, are weak defensively but strong offensively.

RUY LOPEZ

White		Black
P — K 4	1	P — K 4
Kt — K B 3	2	Kt — Q B 3
B — Kt 5	3	P — Q R 3
B — R 4	4	Kt — K B 3
O — O	5	Kt × P
P — Q 4	6	P — Q Kt 4
B — Kt 3	7	P — Q 4
P × P	8	B — K 3
P — B 3	9	B — Q B 4 or B — K 2

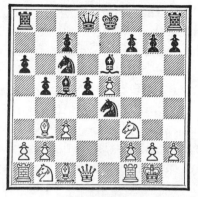

DIAGRAM 76
White to play. Position after Black's 9th move

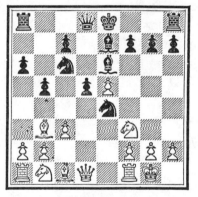

DIAGRAM 77
White to play. Position after Black's 9th move

Black has gained in development but at the expense of a very bad Pawn formation on the Q's wing. Black's Q B P is very backward and experience has shown that with good play White can generally prevent that Pawn from coming up level with his Q Kt P and Q P. If the Q B P cannot come up level with the others then the three White Pawns on the Q's side will hold the four of Black, and the practical result will be that White will be playing as though he were a Pawn to the good, because of his four Pawns to three on the K's side. In this variation White's Pawn at K 5 acts as a wedge against Black's position. Should Black try to get rid of it by P — K B 3, Black's King's side will be weakened, a rather dangerous situation arising because of the fact that on account of the nature of the position Black is practically forced to castle on the K's side. In the position of Diagram 76 the game might continue as follows: 10 Q — K 2, O — O; 11 B — K 3, P — K B 4; 12 P × P e.p., Q × P; 13 Q Kt — Q 2, Kt × Kt; 14 Q × Kt, B × B; 15 Q × B, and White has the better position.

In Diagram 77 the game might continue as follows: 10 Q Kt — Q 2, Kt — B 4; 11 B — B 2, P — Q 5; 12 Kt — K 4, P × P; 13 Kt × Kt, B × Kt; 14 B — K 4, Q — Q 2; 15 P × P, R — Q; 16 Q × Q ch, B × Q; 17 R — Q, Kt — K 2 (Probably best. Black cannot castle because of B — K 3, B × B; R × B, R × R; B × Kt); 18 Kt — Q 4 and White has the advantage. The White P at K 5 restricts the action of Black's pieces, while White has freedom of action. I have had the good fortune of obtaining this position on several occasions in tournament play, and have proved beyond doubt the superiority of White's position.

There are a good many more variations to the Ruy Lopez, but those shown in the text are most in use by the experts. The thing for the student to think about is the general form of development, aiming from the beginning at the control of the centre. The pieces are generally placed on commanding squares, as safe as possible from attack. Care is taken not to move the same piece twice before full development, unless a second move is necessary for some essential purpose. The P formation as well as the resulting greater or lesser mobility of the pieces arising from the opening moves are factors to be borne in mind always. The gain of a single P in the opening will generally produce positive results. For the average player any further discussion of these matters might prove futile.

For the sake of information a single variation is given below of some of the gambits arising from White's second move 2 P — K B 4 or P — Q 4.

KING'S GAMBIT

White		Black
P — K 4	1	P — K 4
P — K B 4	2	P × P
Kt — K B 3	3	P — K Kt 4
B — B 4	4	B — Kt 2

4...P — Kt 5, bringing about the Muzio gambit, is unsafe and unnecessary. The text move gives Black an excellent game.

O — O	5	P — Q 3
P — Q 4	6	Kt — Q B 3
P — Q B 3	7	P — K R 3

In order to play the Kt to K 2 or K B 3 and then castle on the K's side, leaving Black a Pawn ahead with a good game.

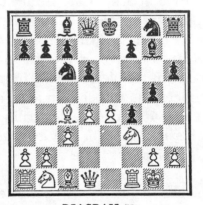

DIAGRAM 78
White to play. Position after Black's 7th move

KING'S BISHOP GAMBIT

White		Black
P — K 4	1	P — K 4
P — K B 4	2	P × P
B — B 4	3	

This is the most difficult gambit to handle. Black may check at K R 5 and prevent White from castling, but in so doing he brings his Q out before any of his minor pieces are in play. There are innumerable complications arising from such play, with the final result always in doubt. Black, however, can avoid all those complications by playing now

3   Kt — K B 3

If now White plays 4 P — K 5, P — Q 4 will give Black a very good open game.

Kt — Q B 3   4   Kt — B 3

Black must be very careful as to the order in which he makes the different moves. The slightest error will bring disaster. The text move prevents P — K 5 at the same time that it brings out a piece into the fray.

P — Q 3   5

Any other move would give Black a decided advantage. Thus if 5 P — Q 4, B — Kt 5 and White has no good defence against the double threat of Kt × P and P — Q 4. If 5 Kt — K B 3, B — Kt 5; 6 O — O, O — O; 7 P — Q 4, P — Q 3 with advantage.

     5   B — Kt 5

DIAGRAM 79

White to play. Position after Black's 5th move

And White has no good move against the threatened advance of the Q P to Q 4. In other words, whether White plays 6 Kt — K 2 or 6 B × P, Black plays

P — Q 4 and gets a free open game with a very solid position.

CENTRE GAME

White		Black
P — K 4	1	P — K 4
P — Q 4	2	P × P
Q × P	3	Kt — Q B 3
Q — K 3	4	Kt — B 3
Kt — Q B 3	5	B — Kt 5
B — Q 2	6	O — O
O — O — O	7	R — K
Q — Kt 3	8	Kt × P
Kt × Kt	9	R × Kt
B — B 4	10	Q — B 3

DIAGRAM 80

White to play. Position after Black's 10th move

Black gives back the Pawn to free his game and take the initiative in accordance with the principles laid down in the text. If White plays B × P, then P — Q 3, shutting off the B and bringing out into play the rest of Black's pieces.

White		Black
Kt — R 3	11	P — Q 3
B — Q 3	12	Kt — Q 5

Black could also play R — K. White's attack could probably be stopped without loss of material. In that case, with a Pawn more, Black's game would have a decided advantage. The text move is more aggressive and therefore more in accord with the theories expounded in this book.

B — K 3	13	R — Kt 5
B × Kt	14	R × B
P — Q B 3	15	B × P
P × B	16	R — K Kt 5
Q — K 3	17	Q × P ch
B — B 2	18	Q × Q
P × Q	19	R × P

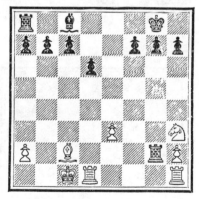

DIAGRAM 81

White to play. Position after Black's 19th move

Black has an excellent chance to win such a position with four Pawns for a Kt. Besides, all the remaining White Pawns are isolated. A very lively variation.

CENTRE GAMBIT

White		Black
P — K 4	1	P — K 4
P — Q 4	2	P × P
P — Q B 3	3	P — Q 4

Black could have taken the Pawn and played one of the several gambits arising from that move, but it is simpler and easier to play according to the text.

K P × P	4	Q × P
P × P	5	Kt — Q B 3
Kt — K B 3	6	B — K Kt 5
B — K 2	7	B — Kt 5 ch
Kt — B 3	8	B × K Kt
B × B	9	Q — B 5
B × Kt ch	10	P × B
Q — K 2 ch	11	Q × Q ch
K × Q	12	O — O — O

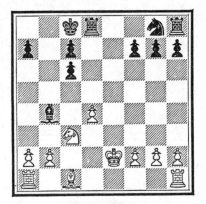

DIAGRAM 82
White to play.   Position after Black's 12th move

And Black, although with a broken Q's side Pawn formation, has an excellent game because White will have trouble in defending his Q P. Black not only has one of his Rooks on the open file, but by playing Kt — K 2 and K R — K he will exert great pressure on the White K and the White Q P, on account of the threat of the Kt *via* K B 4.

There are a good many other gambits but it is not within the scope of this book to study them. The gambits given are those which arise directly from the move P — K 4 followed by either P — K B 4 or P — Q 4. The reader should compare the positions arising from these gambits and those arising from the Ruy Lopez. Probably he will see why it is that the leading experts prefer, with the White pieces, to play the Ruy Lopez rather than any of these gambits.

Let us now take up the openings arising from 1 P — Q 4. The type of game arising from P — Q 4 is generally a so-called close game. The play involved is generally position play only. Position play is the most difficult thing in chess. It is hard to explain and it is hard to understand. Sometimes the choice of move is only a matter of opinion, difficult to prove one way or another. It is for that reason that this opening has been left for the end of the book, hoping that by the time the reader gets to it, his game will have improved enough to warrant his going into the complicated variations arising from P — Q 4.

QUEEN'S GAMBIT

White		Black
P — Q 4	1	P — Q 4

Black could also play Kt — K B 3 or P — K 3 or
P — K B 4 or P — Q B 3 or P — Q B 4 or P — Q 3.
All other moves would be inferior, giving Black a
practically hopeless game from the outset.

P — Q B 4   2

Already there is a dilemma. Should Black take the
P or not? It is not at all certain that the P cannot
be taken, and this may even be Black's best way out
of the dilemma; though at present most of the experts
believe that if Black takes the P, White's development is made easier. Let us therefore not take the
P and look at the two main moves left for Black,
namely P — K 3 or P — Q B 3.

	2	P — K 3
Kt — Q B 3	3	Kt — K B 3
B — Kt 5	4	B — K 2
P — K 3	5	O — O
Kt — B 3	6	Q Kt — Q 2

Other possible defences are 6 P — Q B 3 and P —
Q Kt 3, also Kt — K 5; but they are probably inferior to the variation of the text. In any case it is
our purpose to show one good defence for Black, so
that the student may be on safe ground. Later on
by himself, if he so desires, he may indulge in playing the innumerable variations of this opening. Any
pamphlet or chapter from a book on the Q's opening
will have hundreds of them.

R — Q B   7   P — Q B 3

Black has been developing and preparing to play
P × P as soon as the White K B comes out. In this

way he gains a tempo because the White Bishop will have to move twice in succession. White, on the other hand, does not want to play P × P because it would help the development of Black's Q B. It might be well to state now that the greatest difficulty for Black in the Q's Gambit is the successful development of his Q B.

B — Q 3   8

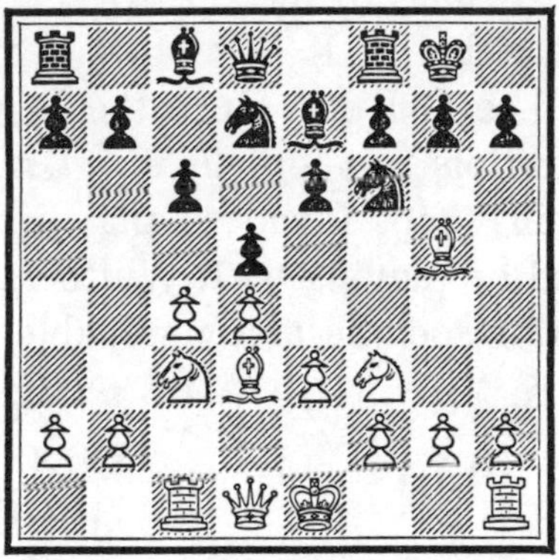

DIAGRAM 83
Black to move. Position after White's 8th move

A look at the position will show that White has better control of the centre and more freedom for his pieces. On the other hand he has not castled yet. Black must now try to free his position before White castles; otherwise his position will gradually get worse. Furthermore, Black wants to get his Q B into play. To be sure, he can play P — Q Kt 3 followed by B — Kt 2, but then his 7 move P — Q B 3 was a lost move. The problem is therefore how to free Black's position without loss of time. The way to do it is as follows:

	8	P × P
B × P	9	Kt — Q 4
B × B	10	Q × B
O — O	11	Kt × Kt
R × Kt	12	P — K 4

For years I played P — Q B 3 with success. I followed it by placing the B at Kt 2, the Q R at Q B, the K R at Q, and then according to the circumstances the P was advanced to Q B 4 or the Kt was first placed either at K B 3 or K B 1 and then the P advanced to Q B 4. Once the P was at Q B 4, Black's position was excellent. Unfortunately at Budapest, in 1929, I had to play against my own system, and by playing with White 13 Q — B 2 the Black position soon became untenable.

P × P	13	Kt × P
Kt × Kt	14	Q × Kt
P — K B 4	15	Q — K 5

DIAGRAM 84

White to play. Position after Black's 15th move

Bogoljuboff's move to prevent the bottling up of Black's Q B. White's idea was to play either P — K 4 or P — B 5, according to Black's move, and thus prevent the B from coming out into play. The text move aims to prevent both those moves of White. If White plays 16 Q — K 2, R — Q; 17 B — Q 3, B — Kt 5! with a good game for Black. If 16 B — Kt 3, B — B 4. White's best move is 16 R — K, against which Black's best answer is probably Q — K 2. It is evident that Black will have some difficulty to come out safely with his B. What else can be done? Let us go back to Diag. 83. In that position Black can first play 8...P — K R 3, preparatory to P × P. We have then

	8	P — K R 3
B — R 4	9	P × P
B × P	10	Kt — Q 4

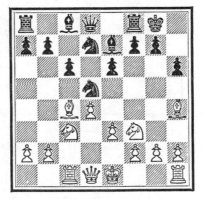

DIAGRAM 85

White to play. Position after Black's 10th move

Now if 11 B × B, Q × B; 12 O — O, Kt × Kt; 13 R × Kt, P — Q Kt 3, and my old system of defence works perfectly because with the P at K R 3 the move 14 Q — B 2 is answered by B — Kt 2 and White cannot gain the all-important *tempo* with

15 B — Q 3. This move, in the old position, with
the P at K R 2, attacked the K R P and gained time
for the attack of the Q B P with the B *via* K 4 or with
the Kt *via* K 5, according to whatever move Black
made.   If in the position of Diag. 85 White plays
B — Kt 3 we have again:

B — Kt 3	11	Kt × Kt
P × Kt	12	P — Q Kt 3
O — O	13	B — Kt 2
Q — K 2	14	Kt — B 3

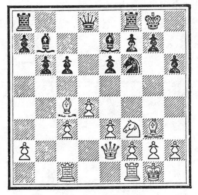

DIAGRAM 86
White to play.   Position after Black's 14th move

A hard game for Black.   White has better control
of the centre and a freer game.   The student will
realize by this time that the great problem in chess is
how to play with the Black pieces against accurate
development on the part of White.   The fact is that
White, having the first move, has the initiative, and
the initiative is an advantage.   The first move also
is a *tempo,* which means time, and time is an element

that has to be considered. In the position of the diagram there are two things that Black must bear in mind in order to get out of his troubles. One is to time the advance of his Q B P, and the other is to get rid of White's Q B at the first good opportunity. Of course if he can get rid of White's K B, then Black will be well off, but this latter chance is very remote. The advance of the Q B P must be made when the move K R — Q on White's part can be safely met. The White Q B may be exchanged by either the Black K B or the Black Kt, according to the circumstances. The advance of Black's Q B P must be timed with care so as not to lose too much time or strengthen White's position too much. This type of game, however, offers many chances for error, and should White overreach himself in pressing his advantage he may suddenly find that his position has taken a turn for the worse, and instead of having the best of it he may confront a situation where he may have to fight for his own life.

There are a good many variations arising from Black's second move P — K 3, but as stated before it is not the purpose of this book to go into all of them. With the variations already shown the student should be able to give a good account of himself. At any rate it is rather doubtful if any of the other variations would prove easier to handle than those shown above. Let us now look at some of those arising from 2...P — Q B 3.

QUEEN'S GAMBIT

White		Black
P — Q 4	1	P — Q 4
P — Q B 4	2	P — Q B 3

This move has the advantage over P — K 3 of keeping open the line of the B. From that point of view it may prove to be a better defence for the reader to follow than those arising from 2...P — K 3.

Kt — K B 3   3   Kt — B 3

Black already threatens to take the P, which he will be able to defend by P — Q Kt 4. It is true that White can always find some way to regain the Pawn, but in order to do so he must lose a lot of time which Black will utilize to develop his game.

White		Black
Kt — B 3	4	P × P
P — Q R 4	5	

White could also play 5 P — K 3 and then would follow P — Q Kt 4; 6 P — Q R 4, P — Kt 5; 7 Kt — Q Kt regaining his Pawn. In this variation Black will place his Q B at Kt 2, his Q Kt at Q 2, and finally advance his Pawn to Q B 4; all this after having played first P — K 3. Sometimes, according to White's play, it is essential to play P — Q R 4 and Q — Kt 3 also before advancing the Pawn to Q B 4. In this way Black obtains a good development. In fact the experts have given up that line of play for White because they think that Black obtains too good a game. Whether that is exact or not it is hard to say. The resulting position is extremely complicated and in any case it will be easier for the student to follow the general trend of the experts, except on the few occasions which it can be proved erroneous. The text move 5 P — Q R 4 is now considered by the experts as the most satisfactory way to develop White's game

5   B — B 4

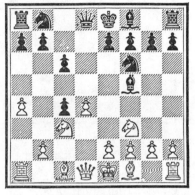

DIAGRAM 87
White to play.   Position after Black's 5th move

The Q B is out, and not only it is out, but it controls the important central square K 4.   Theoretically this should be Black's best form of development.   It certainly is for the average player, and I strongly advise the reader to use this form of defence of the Q's Gambit.   Only when facing experts will they have any trouble, and that trouble they will have always, no matter what form of defence they may adopt. Here they will have all the pieces out, and will not have to struggle, as in the other defences, to get the Q B into play.

Kt — K 5   6

White could also play as follows: 6 P — K 3, P — K 3; 7 B × P, B — Q Kt 5; 8 O — O, O — O; 9 Q — Kt 3 with a good game.

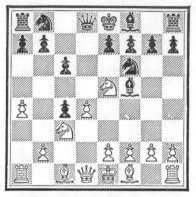

DIAGRAM 88

Black to play. Position after White's 6th move

Black has two distinctly different lines of defence.
He may play P — K 3, whereupon will follow 7 P —
K B 3 for White, with the idea of playing P — K 4,
blocking the action of the Bishop. In this variation
White will retake the P at Q B 4 either with the Kt
or B according to the circumstances, will post his Q B
at K 3 or K Kt 5, then castle and keep as long as he
can the K 4, K B 3, K Kt 2 formation of Pawns in
order to keep Black's Q B from taking an active part
in the game. If White is able to do that long enough
he will have a good chance to win the game since for
all practical purposes he will be playing with a Bishop
more than Black. In order to avoid such a thing
Black may adopt a different line of development beginning with 6...Q Kt — Q 2. Again this is more in
accord with the general theory which states that in
the openings " Pieces should be moved in preference
to Pawns." This means, of course, when there is no
special reason to do otherwise. It might be well to

state here that in close openings this principle does
not apply so regularly as it does in the open game.
Also in close openings the element of time is of less
consequence than in the open game. In the close
openings there is one very predominant factor: PO–
SITION, with MATERIAL a close second. Let us
look at the variation beginning with 6...Q Kt — Q 2.

	White		Black
		6	Q Kt — Q 2
	Kt × P at Q B 4	7	Q — B 2

Black could also play Kt — Kt 3 but he would gain
nothing thereby since the White Kt could go back to
K 5. The text move is made with the idea of playing
P — K 4 immediately and obtaining full development for Black. All this is in accord with the general
principles of development.

White		Black
P — K Kt 3	8	P — K 4
P × P	9	Kt × P
B — B 4	10	K Kt — Q 2
B — Kt 2	11	P — B 3
O — O	12	B — K 3
Kt × Kt	13	P × Kt
B — K 3	14	B — Q B 4

White has gained a little in development, since Black
has not yet castled. White has also the more solid
position, but Black is almost fully developed and if
he can castle without losing too much ground he
should be able to come out of all his troubles. We
have now seen some of the best defences at Black's

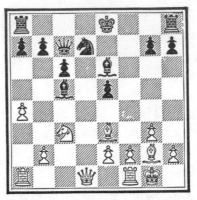

DIAGRAM 89

White to play. Position after Black's 14th move

disposal against the Q's Gambit. For the sake of information two more variations of those mostly in use will be given.

QUEEN'S GAMBIT

White		Black
P — Q 4	1	P — Q 4
P — Q B 4	2	P — K 3
Kt — Q B 3	3	Kt — K B 3
B — Kt 5	4	B — K 2
Kt — B 3	5	O — O
P — K 3	6	Q Kt — Q 2
R — B	7	P — Q Kt 3

With the idea of developing the B *via* Kt 2 and then advancing the Q B P to B 4.

| P × P | 8 | P × P |
| B — Kt 5 | 9 | |

My own invention to obtain full development and at the same time to prevent the advance of Black's Q B P. Other standard moves are B — Q 3 and

Q — R 4. The text move is probably the strongest
of the three.

	9	B — Kt 2
O — O	10	P — Q R 3
B — R 4	11	R — Q B

It would not be safe to advance the Q B P because of
B × Q Kt, Kt × B; B × B, Q × B; P × P, Q × P,
with a decided advantage for White.

B — Kt 3   12

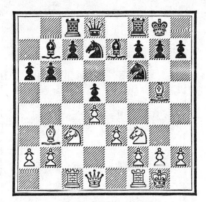

DIAGRAM 90

Black to move. Position after White's 12th move

And if Black advances the Q B P White takes it and
Black is compelled to retake with the Kt in order to
avoid the loss of a Pawn. By retaking with the Kt
Black will be left with an isolated Q P, difficult to
defend, and will have no compensation for it.

QUEEN'S GAMBIT

White		Black
P — Q 4	1	P — Q 4
P — Q B 4	2	P — K 3
Kt — Q B 3	3	P — Q B 4

Recommended by Dr. Tarrasch. It gives Black a rapid and free development, but it leaves him with a weak isolated Q P, which becomes very difficult to defend against accurate play on White's part.

P × Q P	4	K P × P
Kt — B 3	5	Kt — K B 3
P — K Kt 3	6	Kt — B 3
B — Kt 2	7	B — K 2
O — O	8	O — O
P × P	9	B × P
Kt — Q R 4	10	B — K 2
B — K 3	11	

DIAGRAM 91

Black to play. Position after White's 11th move

The Black's Q's Pawn is fixed. White controls the squares Q 4 and Q B 5, and Black will have difficulty in defending the Q P. The bad feature of this variation for Black is that besides having a very difficult game to play, there are not many chances for White to make a serious mistake, because the whole play will centre about the Q P which White will try to win while Black will try to defend it. The type of game involved is very dry, hardly the game that most players would enjoy.

We have now seen some of the leading variations of the Q's Gambit. Again the thing for the average player to consider is the general form of development. It should be stated by this time that the order in which the moves are made in the opening is very important. A change in the order of the moves is apt to bring about a change of the variation to be played, and this change may prove fatal. Great care must therefore be exercised not only in developing the pieces, but in bringing them out in the proper order. The expert sometimes plans from the very first move the type of opening he wishes to play. At other times he is more indifferent about it and is satisfied to obtain one of several types. The leading players, once they have passed the opening stage, will always plan the general form of battle. In making this plan they always consider the type of game they are called upon to play. The plan should, of course, be solid and yet elastic enough to be susceptible of change according to the way the battle develops. The average player cannot be expected to do such a thing, because he has not sufficient vision or knowledge for it; but he can always approach the subject in the same vein. Through care and method and the application of the general principles of the game, he may make up in part at least for his deficiencies.

Let us now look at some of the variations arising from some of the irregular forms of defence against White's first move P — Q 4.

White		Black
P — Q 4	1	Kt — K B 3
P — Q B 4	2	P — K 3
Kt — Q B 3	3	B — Kt 5

There are now a large choice of moves for White, but the two generally in use are Q — Kt 3 and Q — B 2. The last move aims at converting the opening into a sort of Q's Gambit, the first move forces the game into entirely different channels. Let us look first at Q — Kt 3.

Q — Kt 3	4	P — Q B 4
P × P	5	Kt — B 3
Kt — B 3	6	Kt — K 5
B — Q 2	7	Kt × Q B P

This Kt has been moved three times before full development has taken place. This is wrong in principle, but then it should be remembered that this is a close game where the element of time is not of such vital importance. Also Black regains time by the fact that the last move attacks the Q which has to move away.

White		Black
Q — B 2	8	O — O
P — Q R 3	9	B × Kt
B × B	10	P — Q R 4
P — K Kt 3	11	Q — K 2
B — Kt 2	12	P — K 4
O — O	13	P — R 5

DIAGRAM 92

White to move. From a game Stahlberg-Nimzovitsch. Position after Black's 13th move

P — R 5

White has two Bishops and a solid position. Black
in compensation has a strongly posted Kt at Q B 4.
All things considered, the position seems to be slightly
favourable to White, though probably not favourable
enough to win. This variation is taken from a recent
game Stahlberg-Nimzovitsch, won by White. Since
Nimzovitsch has specialized on this kind of defence,
it must be assumed that there is nothing better for
Black in this variation.

Let us now look at the other variation beginning
with 4 Q — B 2.

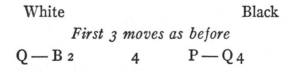

White		Black
First 3 moves as before		
Q — B 2	4	P — Q 4

DIAGRAM 93

White to play. Position after Black's 4th move
P — Q 4

White has now the choice of several moves. Let us examine four of them: P — K 3, B — Q 2, Kt — B 3 and P × P.

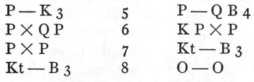

P — K 3	5	P — Q B 4
P × Q P	6	K P × P
P × P	7	Kt — B 3
Kt — B 3	8	O — O

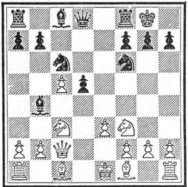

DIAGRAM 94

White to move. Position after Black's 8th move
O — O

A very satisfactory game for Black. He has an isolated P, but is ahead in development. White's fifth
move P — K 3 shuts off the Q B. A move of that
type cannot be a good move unless there is a very
strong reason for it. That not being the case here,
P — K 3 must be considered inferior.

White		Black
P — Q 4	1	Kt — K B 3
P — Q B 4	2	P — K 3
Kt — Q B 3	3	B — Kt 5
Q — B 2	4	P — Q 4
Kt — B 3	5	P × P
B — Q 2	6	P — Q B 3

This is the best move if Black wishes to hold the
Pawn. White can now obtain a good game in two
different ways. He may play P — K Kt 3 followed
by B — Kt 2 and Black will have difficulty in holding his extra P because of the fact that he must advance his Q Kt P to Kt 4 in order to protect his
P at B 5, and then the White B at K Kt 2 will exert
great pressure along the long diagonal. White may
also play as follows: 7 P — K 4, P — Q Kt 4; 8 B —
K 2 followed by castling on the K's side, and White
will have a very strong game in exchange for a Pawn.
Black may, however, avoid all these complications
by not trying to hold the P. On move 6 he may play
P — Q B 4 instead of P — Q B 3, and then we may
have: 7 P — K 3, P — Q R 3; 8 P × P, B × P;
9 B × P, O — O.

DIAGRAM 95

White to play. Position after Black's 9th move

O — O

White is slightly ahead in development, but Black should be able to bring out his pieces gradually until full development is obtained, without losing ground.

Let us go back to move 5 and suppose that White played 5 B — Q 2 and that Black took the Pawn. White could then play Kt — B 3 and we should have exactly one of the positions already examined. If instead of Kt — B 3 White continued with P — K 3 Black would have the choice of trying to hold the P or of playing for development with P — Q B 4. In this case we should arrive to the same position as in Diagram 95. If Black chose to defend his extra Pawn he might get into a hard game. However, the fact that in one way or another Black is able to obtain a rather satisfactory game is proof enough that the moves played for White were not the best. There remains therefore the one move we have not examined, namely 5 P × P. This move is more in accord with the general theory of development. It has the draw-

back of freeing at once Black's Q B, but the fact that
Black has his K B at Q Kt 5 in what comes out to be
a variation of the Q's Gambit should be a compensation for the freeing of his Q B.

In order to understand better this last variation,
which is probably the best system for White against
this form of defence, it might be well to make a halt
and take a look at one of the many variations of the
Q's Gambit that results in a very similar position to
the one we shall have to study.

White		Black
P — Q 4	1	P — Q 4
P — Q B 4	2	P — K 3
Kt — Q B 3	3	Kt — K B 3
B — Kt 5	4	B — K 2
P — K 3	5	Q Kt — Q 2
Kt — B 3	6	O — O
R — Q B	7	P — Q R 3

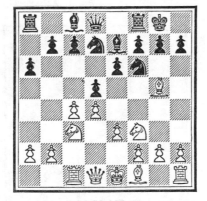

DIAGRAM 96
White to play. Position after Black's 7th move
P — Q R 3

This move was introduced by Henneberger of Switzerland. It involves a very good plan to gain time for development. Instead of P — Q B 3, which is purely defensive, this move is made aiming at a sudden change in tactics in order to assume the initiative. The idea is to play P × P followed by P — Q Kt 4 and B — Kt 2 and finally P — Q B 4, making a demonstration against White's centre and at the same time putting all the Black pieces in play. It is an excellent idea and it proved successful for some time. Experience showed that White could not play P — B 5 with success, and against the normal lines of development the manœuvre P × P, P — Q Kt 4 etc., worked to perfection. This variation was played against the present author a couple of times until I evolved a very simple plan which practically finished the whole system. This plan consisted of playing now, at once, 8 P × P. Black retook with the Pawn, of course, and later on had to play P — Q B 3; thus

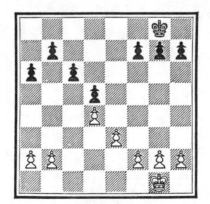

DIAGRAM 97

instead of winning a tempo, Black lost one, since he played both P — Q B 3 and P — Q R 3. This, however, in a close opening is not, as already stated, so very important; but as a result of the manœuvre, the Pawn position in Diagram 97 was arrived at.

This Pawn formation is very interesting and worth a great deal of study to the average player as well as to the expert. (Bear in mind that both Kings are castled on the K's side.) Generally one should act on the side where one has a preponderance of force, but here it is different. Because of the Kings, the advance on the K's side would be extremely dangerous. It is, therefore, on the Q's side where the advance takes place, and it is White that does the advancing. If Black attempted an advance it would only debilitate his Pawn position. P — Q B 4 would leave him with an isolated Q P, and any other advance would be worse. White on the other hand will advance his two Pawns to Q R 4 and Q Kt 4. The one thing White must watch for is the control of his own Q B 4 square, so that Black may not post a Kt there. After White has advanced his Pawns to Q R 4 and Q Kt 4 he will wait for the proper time, and then advance his P to Kt 5. What takes place then? If the Pawns are exchanged at Kt 5, Black will have an isolated backward Q Kt P and an isolated Q P. It certainly would be bad to have two such Pawns to defend, so that will have to be ruled out. What generally takes place is: first an exchange at Kt 5 through R P × P by Black, White retaking, of course; then Black will wait for White to exchange at Q B 3. The result will be a backward weak Pawn for Black at Q B 3, which will be somewhat difficult to defend.

Another very important point in these positions is the fact that in the resultant ending, White remains with his K B against Black's Q B, and under those conditions the position of the Black Pawns at Q 4 and Q B 3 is strategically wrong, because of the fact that Black has these Pawns in the same colour square as his B, while practically all of White's Pawns are on opposite colour squares from that of his own Bishop. The latter is as it should be. The result will be that in the ending the White B will be able to attack the Black Pawns while the Black Bishop will be unable to return the compliment. Because of all these considerations White has theoretically an advantage. Add to this the fact that in such openings White generally wins a little time, because of the solidity of his position, and it will follow, logically, that White must have an advantage.

On the King's side the position is of course reversed, but the fact that the Kings are there and need to be guarded makes it impossible for Black to adopt a similar policy to that of White on the Q's side.

We have purposely tarried on the position above, because of the many principles involved and also to give the reader an insight into the high strategy of chess. Let us now go back to Diagram 93 and examine what takes place after 5 P × P.

White		Black
P × P	5	P × P
B — Kt 5	6	

DIAGRAM 98
Black to play.   Position after White's 6th move
B — Kt 5

Already the possibility of a similar Pawn formation
to that previously studied is evident.   If Black castles, White will play P — K 3 followed by B — Q 3
and Kt — B 3 (or K 2) and O — O.   Then, sooner
or later, Black will have to play P — Q B 3, and we
will have a very similar situation to that previously
examined.   Black may play 6...Q — Q 3 trying to
free his Kt and turn the game into different channels,
but White will reply with P — K 3 and it will be
rather difficult for Black to avoid playing P — Q B 3
at some time or other.   Of course, this does not mean
that P — Q B 3 for Black will bring about a losing
position for Black under all circumstances, but the
point that we wish to emphasize is that by this system of development White is able to force a type of
position generally favourable to the first player.
There is no reason to tarry any longer on these different variations.   The main point is the general aspect of the matter.   General lines are more important

than individual aspects and technicalities. From this variation, however, the reader should arrive at a good understanding of the close relation between the opening, the middle game and the end game. Time after time the expert will decide on a move in the opening because of its resultant effect in a possible ending arising from the game in question. As we close this chapter we hope that the reader has obtained all the information necessary to play a really strong game.

SYNTHESIS OF GENERAL THEORY

Considering the game of chess as a whole divided into three parts, Opening, Middle Game and End Game, the thing to bear in mind is the close interrelation between the component parts of the whole. The End Game being the last part may, to be sure, be considered by itself; but no middle game position should be considered without regard to the possible endings arising from it. In the same manner the Opening should never be considered by itself, but always in connection with the Middle Game and End Game that may arise from it.

If chess were to be considered as a purely scientific study, the endings would have to be thoroughly studied and understood before taking up the middle game. In the same way a complete study and knowledge of the middle game would have to precede the study of the openings. Considered as an intellectual pastime of either an artistic or scientific nature, the matter changes. The majority of those playing the game are mostly interested in combinations and direct attacks against the King. As imagination is needed for that kind of play, such interest should be encouraged. As the player improves other things begin to interest him and the other aspects of the game become more important. A little method, however, from the very beginning will not be amiss and the application of general principles at any time can only help and never detract from the interest of the game.

For the benefit and convenience of our readers a short summary is given below of some of the general principles involved in the different stages of the game.

In the openings we should emphasize:

1. Rapid and solid development, avoiding the creation of any permanent weakness. It follows that if through your development you induce your opponent into creating any such weakness, so much the better. The development should aim at the control of the centre, either through immediate possession of it by the Pawns, or by the long-range action of the pieces.

2. Do not move the same piece twice before full development has taken place.

3. Avoid loss of material without full compensation.

In the middle game:

1. Co-ordinate the action of your pieces.

2. Control of the centre is essential to a successful attack against the King.

3. Direct and violent attacks against the King must be made *en masse*, with full force, to ensure their success. The opposition must be overcome at

all cost; the attack cannot be broken off, because that generally means defeat.

4. Other things being equal, any material gain, no matter how small, means success.

5. Position comes first; material next. Space and Time are complementary factors of Position.

6. If the game will go to an ending for a decision, consider the type of ending to come before exchanging pieces.

In the endings:

1. Time increases in importance in the endings.

2. Two Bishops are better than two Knights.

3. A Bishop is generally better than a Knight, but not always.

4. Rook and Bishop are generally better than Rook and Knight.

5. Queen and Knight are generally better than Queen and Bishop.

6. Pawns are strongest when in line with each other.

7. When the opponent has a Bishop it is generally better to have your Pawns on squares of the same colour as your opponent's Bishop. Whenever you have a Bishop, whether the opponent has also one or not, keep your Pawns on squares of opposite colour to that of your own Bishop.

8. The King, a purely defensive piece during the opening and middle game, very often becomes an offensive piece in the endings. In many endings the King is the deciding factor.

9. In endings of one or two minor pieces the King should generally be marched forward towards the

centre of the board. In King and Pawns endings almost invariably so.

Note. — Those General Principles not in this book will be found in Chess Fundamentals, where all the general principles of chess are expounded in a clear and concise manner.

Part Three

Illustrated Games

PART THREE is not for beginners. By the time the student has reached this part of the book, however, he should be a good average player, and a good average player can derive a great deal of benefit from a close study of the ways and methods of the leading players. The selection of games in part three has been made from among the author's best games in the past thirteen years. Only games against the leading players of the World have been taken. It should be, therefore, a very real selection of games.

In passing, it might be mentioned that at no time in the history of chess have there been more than fifteen ranking first class masters, and that most of the time ten or twelve would be nearer the truth. There have been times before 1900 when the select group of players has not included more than half a dozen names, but in the past thirty years there have always been at least ten players with a right to be classified in the group. Even in this select group there have always been two or three who stood above the rest.

In going over the games in part three the student should recognize through the notes to the games the constant application of the theories and principles expounded in this book. A great deal has been written in the past few years about the Hypermodern School. In the openings, the tactics of some of the so-called hypermodernists are somewhat different

from the tactics formerly used. The strategic principles, however, are the same. Fundamental strategic
principles never change, though their mode of application may not always be the same.

Nothing more need be added, except to express
the hope that the reader in going over the games and
notes may derive from them the pleasure and benefit
that they are intended to give.

1. QUEEN'S GAMBIT DECLINED

(World's Championship Match, Havana, 1921)
Tenth Game of the Match

White: Dr. E. Lasker   Black: J. R. Capablanca

White		Black
P — Q 4	1	P — Q 4
P — Q B 4	2	P — K 3
Kt — Q B 3	3	Kt — K B 3
B — Kt 5	4	B — K 2
P — K 3	5	O — O
Kt — B 3	6	Q Kt — Q 2
Q — B 2	7	

The text move is considered inferior to R — B.
White was probably trying to deviate from the better-
known paths.

| | 7 | P — B 4 |

Considered the best answer to Q — B 2.

| R — Q sq | 8 | Q — R 4 |
| B — Q 3 | 9 | P — K R 3 |

To remove the P from the line of the B and thus gain
time for development. White threatened B × P ch.

B — R 4	10	B P × P
K P × P	11	P × P
B × P	12	Kt — Kt 3
B — Q Kt 3	13	B — Q 2
O — O	14	Q R — B
Kt — K 5	15	

Black: J. R. Capablanca

White: Dr. E. Lasker

DIAGRAM 1

Black to move.   Position after White's 15th move

Kt — K 5

Black has obtained an excellent development. He must now find the way either to exchange the White B at K R 4 for his B at K 2, or to post a piece at Q 4 so as to bring about some exchanges that will simplify the position to some extent. All this must be done while keeping immobile the White Pawn at Q 4. White's weakness is his isolated Q P. On the other hand the central position of the P at Q 4 as compared with the less central position of Black's P at K 3 gives White more space and in consequence more freedom of manœuvre.

15   B — Kt 4

This is a weak move which might have given Black a
great deal of trouble.   Black wanted to gain time in
order to play his Q Kt to Q 4, the pivot square of the
whole position for Black.   It was the wrong idea,
however, as will soon be seen.   The simple and logical
move B — B 3, threatening B — Q 4, would have
given Black an excellent game

K R — K   16   Q Kt — Q 4

Black: J. R. Capablanca

White: Dr. E. Lasker
DIAGRAM 2
White to play.   Position after Black's 16th move
Q Kt — Q 4

At first glance Black seems to have the better position.   Such, however, is not the case.   White could
play 17 Q B × Kt, B × B (not Kt × B because of
Kt — Kt 6 which would give White a winning game
because after P × Kt, R × P regains the piece); 18
B × Kt, P × B; 19 Q — B 5 leaving Black with a
very hard game to defend.

K B × Kt	17	Kt × B
B × B	18	Kt × B
Q — Kt 3	19	B — B 3

The B has to go back to his natural square. This in itself is a condemnation of Black's 15th move.

Kt × B	20	P × Kt

After the smoke of battle has cleared away, the position is slightly in favour of Black. It is true that Black has two isolated Pawns, but owing to the position of the pieces the Black Pawns are less easily attacked than the one isolated Q P of White.

R — K 5	21	Q — Kt 3
Q — B 2	22	K R — Q
Kt — K 2	23	

The alternative would be Kt — R 4. But White does not wish to endanger the safety of his Q P. He therefore adopts the text move, which places the Kt in the best defensive position as regards the Q P.

	23	R — Q 4
R × R	24	B P × R

Black has consolidated his position. He holds the open file, his pieces are very well placed, and the only weak point — the isolated Q R P — cannot be attacked because of the general situation of the pieces. The question is, how can Black get the benefit of all this? From now on the student will do well to study carefully every move up to the end. It is one of Black's best efforts in his whole career, and that

Black: J. R. Capablanca

White: Dr. E. Lasker
DIAGRAM 3
White to play.   Position after Black's 24th move
B P × R

against one of the strongest players the World has
ever seen.

    Q — Q 2   25   Kt — B 4

This keeps two of White's pieces tied up to the defence of the Q P and prevents R — Q B.

    P — Q Kt 3   26   P — K R 4

To prevent P — K Kt 4 at any time, thus keeping
White from ever dislodging the Kt at B 4.

    P — K R 3   27   P — R 5

This makes the position of the Kt at B 4 as strong
as it could be.   In order to dislodge the Kt White will
have to play P — K Kt 4, disrupting his K's side.

    Q — Q 3   28   R — B 3

In order to guard the square Q R 3, thus permitting
the Q to go to Kt 5 without letting the White Q penetrate into Black's position.

K — B   29   P — Kt 3

Since White cannot do anything but mark time,
Black, having all the time at his disposal, prepares
his position before advancing.

Q — Kt   30   Q — Kt 5
K — Kt   31   P — R 4
Q — Kt 2   32   P — R 5

Black: J. R. Capablanca

White: Dr. E. Lasker
DIAGRAM 4
White to play.   Position after Black's 32d move
P — R 5

By the advance on the Q's side, Black not only re-
moves his only weakness, the isolated Q R P, but he
creates a new weakness in White's game, since White
will soon have another isolated Pawn besides his Q P.
The text move threatens to win a Pawn by R — Kt 3.

Q — Q 2   33

White decides to exchange Queens, hoping thereby to increase his chances of drawing.

	33	Q × Q
R × Q	34	P × P
P × P	35	R — Kt 3
R — Q 3	36	

Forced. If R — Kt 2, R — Kt 5 would win a Pawn.

	36	R — R 3
P — K Kt 4	37	

Without Queens on the board the disrupting of the K's side is not so dangerous. Besides White had to give his King some breathing space.

	37	P × P e.p.
P × P	38	R — R 7
Kt — B 3	39	R — Q B 7
Kt — Q	40	Kt — K 2

Now the Kt comes to the other side to win one of the two weak isolated Pawns. White cannot advance his P to Q Kt 4 because of R — B 8 followed by R — Kt 8.

Kt — K 3	41	R — B 8 ch
K — B 2	42	Kt — B 3
Kt — Q	43	R — Kt 8

The very tempting Kt — Kt 5 would not be so good. For instance 43...Kt — Kt 5; 44 R — Q 2, R — Kt 8; 45 Kt — Kt 2, R × Kt; 46 R × R, Kt — Q 6 ch; 47 K — K 2, Kt × R; 48 K — Q 2 and draws.

Black: J. R. Capablanca

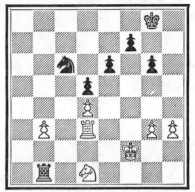

White: Dr. E. Lasker

DIAGRAM 5

White to play. Position after Black's 43d move
R — Kt 8

There is no way for White to save his Q Kt P.
White's next move is not, therefore, a blunder. He
might have played now 44 K — K, Kt — R 4; 45
K — Q 2, R × P; 46 R × R, Kt × R; and there
would have resulted a rather difficult Kt ending,
which should nevertheless be won for Black.

K — K 2	44	R × P
K — K 3	45	R — Kt 5

Having his choice, Black prefers this ending to the
more simple Kt ending.

Kt — B 3	46	Kt — K 2
Kt — K 2	47	Kt — B 4 ch
K — B 2	48	P — Kt 4
P — Kt 4	49	Kt — Q 3
Kt — Kt	50	Kt — K 5 ch
K — B	51	R — Kt 8 ch

K — Kt 2	52	R — Kt 7 ch
K — B	53	R — B 7 ch
K — K	54	R — Q R 7

All these moves with the Rook have had for object to obtain this particular position.

K — B	55	K — Kt 2

The White pieces are practically tied up as a result of the last few moves. Black can now take his time in arriving with his King at the place where he may want to go.

R — K 3	56	K — Kt 3
R — Q 3	57	P — B 3
R — K 3	58	K — B 2
R — Q 3	59	K — K 2
R — K 3	60	K — Q 3
R — Q 3	61	R — B 7 ch

Again the Rook moves have a definite object, and that is to have the same position as before but with the White Rook at K 3, so as to facilitate the advance of the Pawns. Black could, of course, have won without these moves, but it would have taken longer.

K — K	62	R — K Kt 7
K — B	63	R — Q R 7
R — K 3	64	P — K 4
R — Q 3	65	P × P
R × P	66	K — B 4
R — Q	67	P — Q 5
R — B ch	68	K — Q 4

Resigns.

2. QUEEN'S GAMBIT DECLINED

(World's Championship Match, Havana, 1921)
Eleventh Game of the Match

White: J. R. Capablanca   Black: Dr. E. Lasker

White		Black
P — Q 4	1	P — Q 4
Kt — K B 3	2	P — K 3
P — B 4	3	Kt — K B 3
B — Kt 5	4	Q Kt — Q 2
P — K 3	5	B — K 2
Kt — B 3	6	O — O
R — B	7	R — K

At the present time considered inferior to P — Q B 3.

White		Black
Q — B 2	8	P — B 3
B — Q 3	9	P × P
B × P	10	Kt — Q 4
B × B	11	R × B

This was probably the idea behind 7...R — K. It is evident from the development that Black had planned to play very much the kind of game that he obtained. The whole thing reminds one of Steinitz.

White		Black
O — O	12	Kt — B
K R — Q	13	B — Q 2
P — K 4	14	Kt — Q Kt 3
B — B	15	R — B
P — Q Kt 4	16	B — K

The defensive position is Steinitzian in its character, with most of the pieces massed on the last two rows.

Black: Dr. E. Lasker

White: J. R. Capablanca

DIAGRAM 6

White to play.   Position after Black's 16th move

B — K

There are no weak points in Black's game, but the Black position suffers from lack of space for his pieces to manœuvre.   White's policy should be therefore to keep the black pieces within their restricted territory, so that, sooner or later, in order to free them, Black may be forced to make a move that will weaken his structure.   White may also take advantage of the fact that the Black squares Q B 5 and Q 6 are not easily guarded, and try to place his Knights in those squares.   In order to place a Kt at Q 6 White must first play P — K 5.   This advance must be well timed, keeping in mind all the time that it will create a permanent weakness, by establishing a backward Q P at Q 4.   It will also create a hole at Black's Q 4 where the Black pieces may be strongly posted, especially the Knights.   In the position of the diagram White must be on the lookout also for P — B 3, which would permit the Black Bishop to go to K R 4, pinning the Kt at K B 3 and indirectly increasing the pressure against White's Pawn at Q 4.

| Q — Kt 3 | 17 | R (K 2) — B 2 |
| P — Q R 4 | 18 | |

In order to drive back the Kt, so as to have the Black pieces crowd each other.

	18	Kt — Kt 3
P — R 5	19	Kt — Q 2
P — K 5	20	P — Kt 3

White has absolute control of the Black Q 6 square, so Black prepares for an eventual advance of his Q B P to B 4. It is evident that Black's position is very cramped, but it is not easy to see how to obtain a definite advantage for White.

| Kt — K 4 | 21 | R — Kt |

Black: Dr. E. Lasker

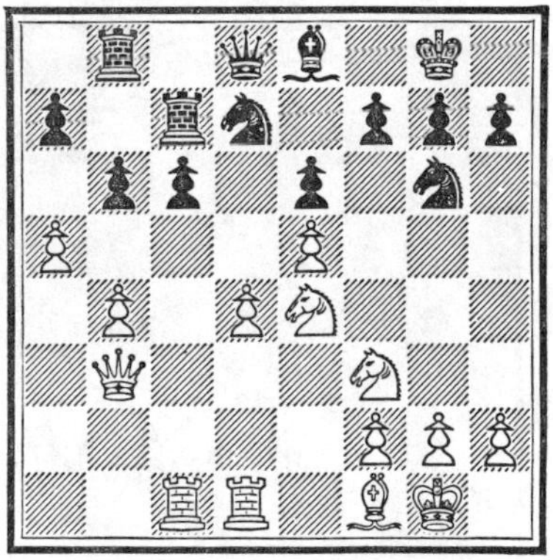

White: J. R. Capablanca

DIAGRAM 7

White to play. Position after Black's 21st move
R — Kt

The position is very interesting. But what is there to be done? Possibly the best move now would be P — R 6 followed by Kt — Q 6, but that simply means that in his previous move Black should have played first P × P before playing R — Kt. The only move that covers all these points is Q — R 3. White, however, failed to make it and as a result Black managed to come out rather well from this position.

Q — B 3	22	Kt — B 5

The result of White's last move; the Black Kt comes into Q 4 with a tempo.

Kt — Q 6	23	Kt — Q 4
Q — R 3	24	P — B 3
Kt × B	25	Q × Kt
P × B P	26	P × B P
P — Kt 5	27	

Black: Dr. E. Lasker

White: J. R. Capablanca

DIAGRAM 8

Black to play. Position after White's 27th move
P — Kt 5

The exposed position of the Black King is rather in-
viting for an attack, but before going into it White
must liquidate his Q's side Pawns in order to remove
all possible sources of weakness.   Once those two
Pawns are exchanged, White can devote all his attention to the attack against the King without having
anything to worry about on the other side.

27   R (Kt) — B

Black's next few moves are practically forced.   Here,
for instance, 27...P — Q B 4 would be met with 28
P × P, P × P; 29 B — B 4 and Black's position
would be untenable.

P × B P	28	R × P
R × R	29	R × R
P × P	30	P × P

After all these exchanges, Black's only compensation
for the exposed condition of his K is the passed
Q Kt P, but the White B prevents its advance.

R — K	31

Possibly B — Kt 5 first, driving back the R to B 2,
was a better way to continue the game.

	31	Q — Q B
Kt — Q 2	32	Kt — B

R — B 6 would not do because of Q — R.

Kt — K 4	33	Q — Q
P — R 4	34	

Black: Dr. E. Lasker

White: J. R. Capablanca
DIAGRAM 9
Black to move.　Position after White's 34th move
P — R 4

There is much more than meets the eye in this position. This is a crucial point in the game. Apparently
there is not much on either side, yet if Black can save
the game it must be done at this point, and the
chances are that the only move that may save the
situation is P — R 3, threatening to drive the Kt
away with P — B 4. 34...P — B 4 at once would
not do because of 35 B — Kt 5, R — B 2; 36 Kt —
Kt 5, R — K 2; 37 B — B 4 and Black would be
helpless. The situation is most interesting and will
repay study.

34　　R — B 2

A natural enough move, yet it will be seen that Black
seems lost from now on.

Q — Kt 3　　35　　R — K Kt 2

White was threatening B — B 4 followed by B × Kt

and Q × P ch. The text move is made to induce White to play P — Kt 3, thus taking that square away from the White Q, which otherwise would always be threatening that check while roaming from one side of the board to the other.

P — Kt 3	36	R — R 2
B — B 4	37	R — R 4
Kt — B 3	38	Kt × Kt

Forced. Now that this Kt has been removed from Q 4 the danger of Black's position becomes clearer.

Q × Kt	39	K — B 2
Q — K 3	40	Q — Q 3
Q — K 4	41	R — R 5
Q — Kt 7 ch	42	K — Kt 3
Q — B 8	43	Q — Kt 5
R — Q B	44	

Black: Dr. E. Lasker

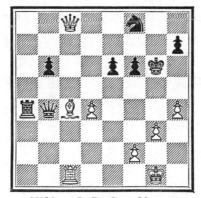

White: J. R. Capablanca
DIAGRAM 10
Black to move. Position after White's 44th move
R — Q B

In this position Black played Q — K 2 and four moves later it was all over. But no matter what Black may play, the end is near at hand. For instance 44...Q — R 6 (probably best); 45 B — Q 3 ch, P — B 4 (Best. Not 45...Q × B because of Q — K 8 ch winning the Rook, nor 45...K — R 3 because of R — B 7 threatening Q × Kt followed by R × P mate); 46 Q — K 8 ch, K — R 3; 47 R — K, R — R; 48 R × P ch, Kt × R; 49 Q × Kt ch, K — Kt 2; 50 Q — K 5 ch and mate in a few more moves.

	44	Q — K 2
B — Q 3 ch	45	K — R 3
R — B 7	46	R — R 8 ch
K — Kt 2	47	Q — Q 3
Q × Kt ch	48	Resigns.

3. QUEEN'S GAMBIT DECLINED

(International Masters Tournament, London, 1922)

White: J. R. Capablanca   Black: Dr. M. Vidmar

P — Q 4	1	P — Q 4
Kt — K B 3	2	Kt — K B 3
P — B 4	3	P — K 3
Kt — B 3	4	B — K 2
B — Kt 5	5	Q Kt — Q 2
P — K 3	6	O — O
R — B	7	P — B 3
Q — B 2	8	

B — Q 3 is considered stronger nowadays.

	8	P × P
B × P	9	Kt — Q 4
B × B	10	Q × B
O — O	11	P — Q Kt 3

A bad move which gets Black into all sorts of trouble. It is essential to play Kt × Kt before making the text move.

Black: Dr. M. Vidmar

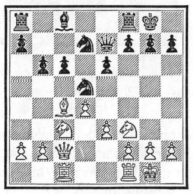

White: J. R. Capablanca
DIAGRAM 11
White to play.   Position after Black's 11th move
P — Q Kt 3

Kt × Kt	12	B P × Kt

Of course not K P ×Kt because of B — Q 3 winning a Pawn.

B — Q 3	13	P — K R 3

Kt — K B 3 would have been better.   Black wants to retard this move so as to prevent Kt — K 5.

Q — B 7	14	Q — Kt 5

Black: Dr. M. Vidmar

White: J. R. Capablanca

DIAGRAM 12

White to play.   Position after Black's 14th move
Q — Kt 5

Black is so much behind in development that this
inroad with the lonesome Q is bound to meet with
failure. His idea is to worry White on the Q's side.
Of course if White should play P — Q Kt 3 then the
Black Queen would be beautifully placed, and if
White now played R — B 2, he could play Kt — B 3
and try to come out with his B. The text move,
however, offers White the opportunity to make a very
fine combination which wins by force.

P — Q R 3   15   Q — R 5

If Q × P, 16 R — Kt, Q × R P; 17 B — Kt 5,
Q — K 2 (Best; if Kt — B 3, 18 R — R, Q — Kt 5;
19 K R — Kt and the Q has no place to go); 18
B — B 6, R — Kt; 19 Kt — K 5, Q — Q; 20
Q × R P, Kt × Kt; 21 P × Kt and Black must lose
a piece.

P — R 3	16	Kt — B 3
Kt — K 5	17	B — Q 2
B — B 2	18	Q — Kt 4
P — Q R 4	19	Q × Kt P
Kt × B	20	

Not the best. R — Kt would have won a piece. Failure to make this move cost White a very good chance to obtain the special prize for the most brilliant game of the tournament.

	20	Q R — B
Q — Kt 7	21	Kt × Kt
B — R 7 ch	22	K × B
R × R	23	R × R
Q × R	24	Kt — B 3

Black has a Pawn for the exchange. In order to win, White must get his Rook into the game. This must be done while taking care at the same time that the Kt be kept back from K 5 — which can be done because Black cannot afford to exchange Queens.

R — B	25	Q — Kt 5

White threatened to play Q — B 2 ch exchanging Queens.

Q — B 2 ch	26	K — Kt
Q — B 6	27	Q — R 6

White is now ready to go after the K and by constantly threatening mate he will be able to prevent the Q and Kt from working together for a while.

Black: Dr. M. Vidmar

White: J. R. Capablanca
DIAGRAM 13
White to play.   Position after Black's 27th move
Q — R 6

Q — R 8 ch	28	K — R 2
R — B 7	29	Q × R P

Black could not defend his K B P.   If K — Kt 3, 30
Q × R P and in order to defend the K B P the Q
would have to retreat to K B, which would be immediately fatal.

R × B P	30	Q — Q 8 ch
K — R 2	31	Q — R 4
Q × R P	32	Q — Kt 3
R — B 8	33	Q — B 4
R — B 7	34	Q — Kt 3
R — Kt 7	35	Kt — K 5
Q — R 2	36	P — K 4
Q × P	37	P × P
R — Kt 8	38	Kt — B 3
Q × P	39	Q — B 4

R × P	40	Q × P
Q — Q 3 ch	41	K — Kt
R — Kt 8 ch	42	Resigns

For after K — B 2, 43 R — Kt 7 ch, K — K 3 (If K — Kt, Q — Kt 6); 44 R × P.

4. RUY LOPEZ

(International Masters Tournament, London, 1922)

White: J. R. Capablanca   Black: E. D. Bogoljuboff

P — K 4	1	P — K 4
Kt — K B 3	2	Kt — Q B 3
B — Kt 5	3	P — Q R 3
B — R 4	4	Kt — B 3
O — O	5	B — K 2
R — K	6	P — Q Kt 4
B — Kt 3	7	P — Q 3
P — B 3	8	O — O
P — Q 4	9	P × P

In the part of the book dealing with the openings it has already been stated that this and the subsequent moves are Bogoljuboff's idea of the best way to play this variation for Black.

P × P	10	B — Kt 5
B — K 3	11	Kt — Q R 4
B — B 2	12	Kt — B 5
B — B	13	P — B 4
P — Q Kt 3	14	Kt — Q R 4
B — Kt 2	15	Kt — B 3
P — Q 5	16	Kt — Kt 5

Black has accomplished his object: to exchange the Kt for one of White's Bishops. The opening has taken a different course from that indicated in our chapter on the openings. This is due to the fact that White chose a line of play not so strong as the one recommended in that chapter. This was the first time that White had to face this variation and he therefore played with a little too much caution to avoid falling into what might have been a prepared trap.

Q Kt — Q 2	17	Kt × B	
Q × Kt	18	R — K	

Kt — Q 2 at once would have been better.

Q — Q 3	19

White should have played P — Q R 4 at once in order to keep Black occupied on the Q's side, or, should he play P — Kt 5, to have a hole for the Kt at Q B 4.

19	P — K R 3

Black must have had a different plan in mind from the one he carried out in the actual game; otherwise this move could not be explained. Again Kt — Q 2 was better.

Kt — B	20	Kt — Q 2	
P — K R 3	21		

This is the turning point of the game. Black should have taken the Kt with the Bishop and then played B — B 3. Failure to do this was the cause of his de-

Black: E. D. Bogoljuboff

White: J. R. Capablanca

DIAGRAM 14

Black to move. Position after White's 21st move
P — K R 3

feat. It may be that Black did not expect White to
follow the bold course which he adopted in the game.

21   B — R 4

From now on this B will be cut out of the game.

K Kt — Q 2	22	B — B 3
B × B	23	Q × B
P — Q R 4	24	P — Q B 5

This move gives Black a passed Pawn, but on the
other hand it helps White to carry out his purpose of
blocking off the B at R 4.

P × B P	25	Kt — B 4
Q — K 3	26	P × R P
P — B 4	27	Q — K 2
P — Kt 4	28	B — Kt 3
P — B 5	29	

The B is completely shut off from the game. From now on till near the end of the game White will be playing practically as though he were a piece ahead. It is true that White's Pawn formation is the worst ever, but a piece more to play with can cover a lot of sins.

		29	B — R 2
Kt — K Kt 3		30	Q — K 4

Quite rightly Black occupies this square with his Q. Apart from the commanding position of the Q, this move precludes any possibility of White playing P — K 5.

		31	Q R — Kt
K — Kt 2			
Q R — Kt		32	P — B 3

To give the K some air. Also to provide against P — K 5 after the Q leaves the square K 4. Besides,

Black: E. D. Bogoljuboff

White: J. R. Capablanca
DIAGRAM 15
White to play.   Position after Black's 32d move
P — B 3

the move prepares for the ultimate re-entrance of the B in the game *via* Kt 1, K B 2, etc. The drawback is that it creates a hole at K 6 for one of the White Knights. However, there was not very much that Black could do in order to avoid the disadvantage arising from such a poor Pawn formation.

Kt — B 3   33

The time has come for White to dislodge the Black pieces from their strongholds.

	33	R — Kt 7 ch
R × R	34	Q × R ch
R — K 2	35	Q — Kt 6
Kt — Q 4	36	Q × Q

Practically forced, since he could not afford to play Q × P because of R — B 2 followed by Kt — K 6. After the exchange of Queens, White's only problem will be to look out for the passed Q R P.

	37	R — Kt
R × Q	38	K — B 2
R — Q B 3	39	R — Kt 7
K — B 3	40	B — Kt
Kt — (Kt 3) — K 2	41	
Kt — K 6		

White plays on the assumption that Black cannot afford to exchange his Kt because of the bad position of his B. If Kt × P, K × Kt, R × Kt ch, K — Q 3, R — R 7, K — Q 4, P — K R 4, P — B 5.

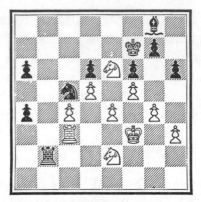

DIAGRAM 16

Black to move.   Position after White's 41st move Kt — K 6

	41	Kt — Kt 6
P — B 5	42	P × P
Kt × B P	43	Kt — Q 7 ch
K — B 2	44	K — K 2

Black might have tried Kt — Kt 8, 45 Kt × P (at R 5), Kt × R; 46 Kt × R, Kt × P ch; 47 K — K 3, Kt — Q 3, with good chances to draw.

K — K	45	Kt — Kt 8

Now White cannot play as before, but the presence of the K at K 2 gives him the opportunity for a combination that will win in a few moves.

R — Q 3	46	P — R 6
P — Q 6 ch	47	K — Q
Kt — Q 4	48	R — Kt 3
Kt — (Q 4) — K 6 ch	49	B × Kt

At last the Bishop comes out but only as a stepping-stone for White's Pawns.

P × B	50	R — Kt
P — K 7 ch	51	K — K
Kt × P	52	Resigns

An exciting game from move 24 to the finish.

5. QUEEN'S GAMBIT ACCEPTED

(International Masters Tournament, Moscow, 1925)

White: J. R. Capablanca   Black: E. D. Bogoljuboff

P — Q 4	1	P — Q 4
P — Q B 4	2	P — K 3
Kt — K B 3	3	P × P
P — K 4	4	P — Q B 4

Kt — K B 3 instead of the text move deserved consideration.

B × P	5	P × P
Kt × P	6	Kt — K B 3
Kt — Q B 3	7	B — B 4
B — K 3	8	

As a result of the system of development adopted by Black, White has gained a move. White has already developed both his Knights and his Bishops while Black has developed only one Kt and one B. In a fairly open position like this, such a thing generally leads to loss of some sort. Black is already hard pressed to find a satisfactory move. If 8...O — O; 9 P — K 5, Kt — Q 4; 10 B × Kt, P × B; 11 O — O with a decided advantage for White.

	8	Q Kt — Q 2

Black wanted to prevent P — K 5. He could not play P — K 4 because of K Kt — Kt 5. The text

move offers White the opportunity of making a most
unusual combination: the sacrifice of a piece early
in the game, before full development has taken place.

Black: E. D. Bogoljuboff

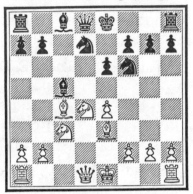

White: J. R. Capablanca
DIAGRAM 17
White to play.   Position after Black's 8th move
Q Kt — Q 2

B × P	9	P × B
Kt × P	10	Q — R 4

The alternative was Q — Kt 3.   White might then
have played 11 Kt × B, Kt × Kt; 12 O — O and
Black would have extreme difficulty to guard against
White's many threats.   For instance: 12...Q — B 3;
13 R — Q B, Q Kt × P; 14 Kt × Kt, Q × Kt; 15
R — K, K — B 2; 16 R — B 7 ch, K — Kt 3; 17
B — Q 4, Q — B 5; 18 R — (K) — K 7, R — Q;
19 R × P ch, K — R 3; 20 R × P ch, Kt × R; 21
R × Kt ch, K × R; 22 Q — R 5 ch, K — Kt; 23
Q — Kt 6 ch, K — B; 24 B — B 5 ch wins.

O — O	11	B × B
P × B	12	K — B 2
Q — Kt 3	13	K — Kt 3
R — B 5	14	

R — B 3 would probably win also, but the text move is better and should have brought about a quick ending.

	14	Q — Kt 3
Kt — B 4 ch	15	K — R 3

Black: E. D. Bogoljuboff

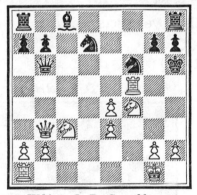

White: J. R. Capablanca

DIAGRAM 18

White to play.   Position after Black's 15th move
K — R 3

White had practically a forced mate thus: 15 Q — B 7, P — Kt 3; 16 P — K Kt 4, Q × P ch; 17 K — Kt 2, P × R; 18 P — Kt 5 ch, K × P; 19 Q — Kt 7 ch, K × Kt; 20 R — B ch, K — K 4; 21 Q — K 7 ch, K — Q 5; 22 R — Q ch, K — B 5; 23 Q — K 6 ch, K — B 4; 24 P — Kt 4 ch, K × P; 25 Q — Kt 3 ch, K moves; 26 Q — Kt 5 mate.

Again: 15 Q — B 7, P — Kt 3; 16 P — K Kt 4, Q × P ch; 17 K — Kt 2, Kt × Kt P (if Kt × K P, Kt — K 6); 18 R — R 5 ch, P × R; 19 Q × P (R 5) ch, K — Kt 2; 20 Q × Kt ch, K — B; 21 Kt — K 6 ch, K — K; 22 Q — R 5 ch, K — K 2; 23 Kt — Q 5 ch winning the Queen. In the actual game White played differently. He thought that he could force the game, without having to go into all these complications, by playing 16 P — K Kt 4, which proved to be a serious mistake.

        P — K Kt 4   16   P — Kt 4

This simple move upsets the cart.

        Q × Q   17   P × Q

        Q R — Q   18

Black: E. D. Bogoljuboff

White: J. R. Capablanca

DIAGRAM 19

Black to play. Position after White's 18th move
Q R — Q

Although Black is a piece ahead he still has trouble to get out of this position without serious loss. He should have simplified the game now by 17...P × Kt 18 P Kt 5 ch, K — Kt 2 (best); 19 P × Kt ch, Kt × P; 20 R — Kt 5 ch, K — B 2; 21 P × P and White would have to fight hard to obtain a draw. Black failed to take advantage of the one chance he had in the whole game.

	18	R — K Kt
K Kt — Q 5	19	Kt × Kt P
Kt — K 7	20	R — Kt 2
R — Q 6 ch	21	K — R 4
R — B 3	22	K Kt — B 3
R — R 3 ch	23	K — Kt 5
R — Kt 3 ch	24	K — R 4
Kt — B 5	25	R — Kt 3

Black: E. D. Bogoljuboff

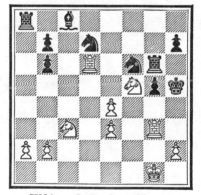

White: J. R. Capablanca

DIAGRAM 20

White to play. Position after Black's 25th move

R — Kt 3

The position is most interesting. Black is in a mating net, but to finish the work is most difficult. Incidentally, all the commentators have gone wrong in their analysis of this position. They have suggested several ways of playing to force a win, but against their suggestions there are ways of getting out. There is in fact only one way to win by force and that is to play now 26 R — R 3 ch. White actually played Kt — K 7 in order to gain time; figuring that Black could not do any better than to come back to this position. Black, however, considering this position as lost, tried to get out by giving up the exchange, and lost. Let us see the variations arising from 26 R — R 3 ch. We have then: K — Kt 5; 27 K — Kt 2; Kt × P; 28 R — Q 5, Kt × Kt; 29 R — R 4 ch, P × R; 30 Kt — R 6 ch, R × Kt; 31 P — R 3 mate. Again: 26 R — R3 ch, K — Kt 5; 27 K — Kt 2, Kt — B 4; 28 Kt — R 6 ch, R × Kt; 29 R × R, Kt — (B 4) × P; 30 Kt × Kt, Kt × Kt; 31 R — Q 5 and Black is lost because of P — K R 3. A most remarkable position.

Kt — K 7	26	P — Kt 5

In order to get his King out of the mating net.

Kt × R	27	K × Kt

If P × Kt, P — K 5.

R × P ch	28	K — B 2
R — B 4	29	K — Kt 2
P — K 5	30	Kt — K
R — K 6	31	Resigns.

After Kt — B 2; 32 R — K 7 ch followed by P — K 6 wins a piece.

(International Masters Tournament, New York, 1927)

White: J. R. Capablanca   Black: Dr. M. Vidmar

White		Black
P — K 4	1	P — K 4
Kt — K B 3	2	Kt — Q B 3
B — Kt 5	3	P — Q R 3
B — R 4	4	Kt — B 3
O — O	5	B — K 2
R — K	6	P — Q Kt 4
B — Kt 3	7	P — Q 3
P — B 3	8	Kt — Q R 4

One alternative in this variation is Bogoljuboff's idea, viz: 8...O — O; 9 P — Q 4, P × P; 10 P × P, B — Kt 5. What is to be done in that case has been discussed in the chapter on the openings.

B — B 2	9	P — B 4
P — Q 4	10	Q — B 2

This move is made with the object of making room for the Kt when White plays as in the text. It involves a rather complicated manœuvre of doubtful value.

Q Kt — Q 2	11	O — O
P — K R 3	12	Kt — B 3

This is all in accord with the original plan of Black. The alternative would be to play 12...K Kt — Q 2 followed by Kt — Kt 3 with the idea of transferring the activities of the Black pieces to the Q's side.

P — Q 5	13	Kt — Q
P — Q R 4	14	P — Kt 5

The alternative would be R — Kt, which, after 15 P × P, P × P, would leave the control of the open Q R file to White. The text move has the drawback of leaving too many holes for the White pieces.

Kt — B 4   15

In this variation this Kt generally goes around *via* K B to either K Kt 3 or K 3 according to the circumstances, but the development of this particular game makes it possible and advisable to veer to the left with this Kt.   An examination of the position will show that the text move is much more aggressive.   It threatens K Kt × P, as actually happened in the game, and also in combination with P — R 5 to work into Black's position.   At the same time it leaves the way open for Kt — K 3 aiming at K B 5, as often occurs in this opening.   The position is a good example of what a good plan should have: enough elasticity for the plan to be changed to advantage at any opportunity.

15   P — Q R 4

Black overlooks the danger.   He is afraid of P — R 5, which would practically force him to play P × P and would leave him rather cramped.   He should submit to it, however, and play 15 ... Kt — K in accord with the whole scheme of the defence, which consists in building a barrier behind the Pawn formation in the centre and on the K's side, and wait for White. The difficulty of the plan lies in the overcrowding of the Black pieces and in the purely defensive nature of the whole system.   Such purely passive resistance

Black: Dr. M. Vidmar

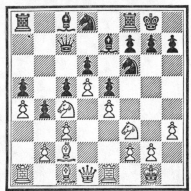

White: J. R. Capablanca
DIAGRAM 21
White to play.   Position after Black's 15th move
P — Q R 4

is not to be recommended except when there is no other choice.   The move 15 ... Kt — K has, however, one other very good feature, and that is the possibility for Black of advancing on the K's side through P — K B 4.

K Kt × P	16	B — R 3
B — Kt 3	17	P × Kt
P — Q 6	18	B × P
Q × B	19	Q × Q
Kt × Q	20	Kt — Kt 2
Kt × Kt	21	B × Kt
P × P	22	B P × P

The smoke of battle has cleared away and the result is even so far as material is concerned; but White has two Bishops and the Black Kt is so placed that it will have difficulty in participating actively in the game

Black: Dr. M. Vidmar

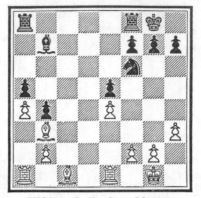

White: J. R. Capablanca
DIAGRAM 22
White to play.   Position after Black's 22d move

for some time.   It is now up to White to take advantage of the element of time combined with the better
position of his pieces, which means really the better
position of his Q B as compared with Black's Kt.

White		Black
P — B 3	23	K R — Q
B — K 3	24	P — R 3
K R — Q	25	B — B 3
Q R — B	26	B — K
K — B 2	27	R × R
R × R	28	R — B
P — Kt 4	29	

White's position is excellent, but he cannot yet try
to win any material, because Black's pieces are too
well placed defensively.   The text move is an advance on the K's side to drive away the Kt from B 3,

in order to be able to play R — Q 5. The idea is, in case Black remains passive, to follow it up with P — R 4 and P — Kt 5 and possibly P — Kt 6. White cannot yet play B — Kt 6, because of Kt — Q 2 followed, if White plays B × P, by Kt — B 4. White's advance, in fact, compels Black to declare himself.

	29	B — Q 2
B — Kt 6	30	B — K 3
B × B	31	P × B
R — Q 8 ch	32	R × R
B × R	33	Kt — Q 2
B × P	34	Kt — B 4
P — Kt 3	35	Kt × Kt P
B × P	36	Kt — Q 5
P — R 5	37	Resigns

6. QUEEN'S GAMBIT DECLINED

(International Masters Tournament, New York, 1927)

White: J. R. Capablanca		Black: R. Spielmann
P — Q 4	1	P — Q 4
Kt — K B 3	2	P — K 3
P — Q B 4	3	Kt — Q 2
Kt — Q B 3	4	K Kt — B 3
B — Kt 5	5	B — Kt 5

Not to be recommended. The move is wrong in principle, because it involves an early counter-attack without sufficient development to justify it. The results will soon be felt.

P × P	6	P × P
Q — R 4	7	B × Kt

Practically forced to avoid the loss of a Pawn. The
fact that this B has to be exchanged for the Kt so
early in the game, leaving White with two Bishops
and a very strong position, is sufficient evidence that
Black's system of development is wrong.   It never
pays to move a B twice in the opening to exchange it
for a Kt, unless some definite advantage is obtained.

P × B	8	O — O
P — K 3	9	P — B 4
B — Q 3	10	P — B 5
B — B 2	11	Q — K 2

Already the absence of Black's K B is being felt. The
Queen has to protect the black squares.

| O — O | 12 | P — Q R 3 |
| K R — K | 13 | |

Black: R. Spielmann

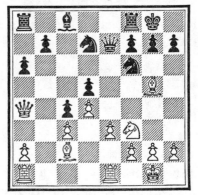

White: J. R. Capablanca
DIAGRAM 23
Black to move.   Position after White's 13th move
K R — K

White threatens P — K 4, breaking up Black's game. Black must stop it. He cannot play 13..P — Q Kt 4; because of 14 Q — R 5, B — Kt 2; 15 Q — B 7 threatening the B and also B × Kt. The fact is that White is fully developed while Black is behind in time, besides having a precarious position. Under the circumstances Black evolves a very clever plan, which almost succeeded in getting him out of his difficulties.

	13	Q — K 3
Kt — Q 2	14	P — Q Kt 4
Q — R 5	15	

This move is the Key to the situation. White was aware of Black's plan beginning with 13..Q – K 3, and prepared a combination to destroy the whole scheme.

	15	Kt — K 5

This is the key to Black's plan. He wants to prevent P — B 3 either before or after P — Q R 4.

Kt × Kt	16	P × Kt
P — Q R 4	17	Q — Q 4

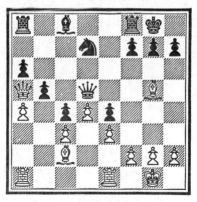

DIAGRAM 24

White to move. Position after Black's 17th move Q — Q 4

Black naturally expected that White would now protect his Bishop, after which Black would play B — Kt 2 and obtain a very satisfactory game. He failed, however, to consider that his expert opponent was not likely to make things so easy for him.

P × P   18

The key to White's combination and a most unpleasant surprise for Black. White does not need to defend his B and as a result Black's game is completely broken up. There is nothing for Black to do now to avoid disaster.

	18	Q × B
B × P	19	R — Kt

If 19...R — R 2; 20 P — Kt 6, Q × Q; 21 P × R, B — Kt 2 (best); 22 R × Q, B × B; 23 R × P, R — R; 24 R — K 2, B — Kt 2 (best); 25 R — R 5, K — B; 26 R — Kt 2, B — B; 27 R — Kt 4, K — K 2; 28 R × P and White has an overwhelming preponderance of material.

P × P	20	R — Kt 4
Q — B 7	21	Kt — Kt 3
P — R 7	22	B — R 6
K R — Kt	23	R × R ch
R × R	24	P — B 4
B — B 3	25	P — B 5
P × P	26	Resigns.

This game was awarded the special prize for the most brilliant game of the tournament.

7. CARO-KANN DEFENCE

(International Masters Tournament, New York, 1927)

White: A. Nimzovitsch   Black: J. R. Capablanca

P — K 4	1	P — Q B 3
P — Q 4	2	P — Q 4
P — K 5	3	

This is one of the forms of attack in this opening. Nowadays it is considered inferior to either Kt — Q B 3 or P × P. The latter move followed by P — Q B 4 is most in vogue at the present time. Both Kt — Q B 3 and P × P are developing moves that tend to gain time. P — K 5 is more in the nature of a positional move; the P at K 5 acting as a wedge. The drawback to P — K 5 is the immediate liberation of the Black Q B. Also, because of the nature of the forthcoming position, White will exchange his K B for Black's Q B, which as a general rule should not be done except for very definite reasons. In most openings Black has trouble in developing his Q B, while White's K B generally plays a very important part in most of the attacks that develop right out of the openings; hence the reason why it is not advisable for White as a rule to play any system of development involving the exchange of White's K B for Black's Q B.

	3	B — B 4
B — Q 3	4	B × B
Q × B	5	P — K 3

| Q Kt — B 3 | 6 | Q — Kt 3 |
| K Kt — K 2 | 7 | P — Q B 4 |

The safest course would have been Q — R 3 to exchange Queens; or should White move away his Q, then Black's Q would be in command of the White squares along the diagonal R 3 — K B 8, owing to the absence of White's K B. Black, however, wishes to avoid the exchange of Queens, which would facilitate the draw. By this advance the evenly balanced force on both sides is broken up. It might be said that the equilibrium of the position is disrupted. The result in these cases varies. Often, as in this game, there is a struggle on both sides of the board, each player trying to obtain the upper hand on one side while holding the opponent on the other side.

| P × P | 8 | B × P |
| O — O | 9 | |

Black: J. R. Capablanca

White: A. Nimzovitsch

DIAGRAM 25

Black to play. Position after White's 9th move
O — O

Black is a little behind in development, but he has a solid position and can regain a little time by playing either Kt — Q 2 or Kt — Q B 3. Should White answer either of these moves with Q — Kt 3, Black would have the choice of the conservative P — K Kt 3 or the risky K — B, to say nothing of a rather good Pawn sacrifice by Kt — K 2. There are too many possibilities to show them all, but it might be interesting to look at some of them. 9...Kt — Q B 3; 10 Kt — R 4, Q — R 4; 11 Kt × B, Q × Kt; 12 B — K 3 and unless Black plays Q — B 5 forcing the exchange of Queens, White will play 13 P — K B 4 and obtain a very similar position to the one he got in the actual game, but with a certain advantage in time owing to the resulting position of the Black Queen. Again 9...Kt — Q B 3; 10 Q — Kt 3, Kt — K 2; 11 Q × P, R — K Kt; 12 Q × R P, K — Q 2 with a very strong attack for the two Pawns. Against 9...Kt — Q 2; 10 Kt — R 4, Q — B 2; 11 Kt × B, Q × Kt (best, as against Kt × Kt White can play 12 Q — Kt 3, P — K Kt 3; 13 Kt — Q 4 with a good game); 12 B — K 3, Q — B 2; 13 P — K B 4 with a position similar to the one he obtained in the actual game but slightly better. In the position of the diagram Black chose a third move 9...Kt — K 2, with the idea of placing a Kt at K B 4 as quickly as possible.

	9	Kt — K 2
Kt — R 4	10	Q — B 3
Kt × B	11	Q × Kt
B — K 3	12	Q — B 2
P — K B 4	13	Kt — B 4
P — B 3	14	Kt — B 3

At last Black is fully developed and with the possibility of castling on either side open to him. In such positions it is generally better to retard castling as long as possible in order to compel the opponent to guard against both possibilities. Besides, should a general exchange take place, bringing about a Rook ending, the King would then be better placed where it is, right in the centre of the board.

QR—Q   15   P—K Kt 3

This move would have to be made sooner or later. Black really wanted to play P — K R 4, but he was hoping that if he left White the opportunity to play P — K Kt 4 White might be tempted to do so.

P — K Kt 4   16

Black: J. R. Capablanca

White: A. Nimzovitsch
DIAGRAM 26
Black to play. Position after White's 16th move
P — K Kt 4

White has accepted the invitation to drive away the Kt. He probably considered that if he did not drive

away the strongly posted Kt, Black would play
P — K R 4 and then the Kt would be a source of
trouble for the rest of the game. Black had considered other factors before allowing this move. He felt
that after the exchange of the Kt for the B he would
play P — K R 4, forcing White to play P — Kt 5.
As a result White's K B P would be very weak. The
whole K's side would be open to any Black piece able
to enter that territory. It is true that it does not
seem possible for Black to penetrate White's defence,
but Black felt that there would be a way to do it.
His judgement was vindicated, since he was able to
prove that White's stronghold could be conquered
and that the weak K B P, combined with the exposed
position of the White K's side, would be the cause of
White's downfall.

	16	Kt × B
Q × Kt	17	P — K R 4

This forces P — Kt 5; otherwise Black would exchange the P and castle on the Q's side with a very
strong attack which White would probably be unable
to withstand.

P — Kt 5	18	O — O
Kt — Q 4	19	Q — Kt 3
R — B 2	20	Q R — B
P — Q R 3	21	R — B 2
R — Q 3	22	Kt — R 4
R — K 2	23	R — K

White threatened P — B 5 and if K P × P, P — K 6.

White		Black
K — Kt 2	24	Kt — B 3
R — (K 2) — Q 2	25	R — (K) — Q B
R — K 2	26	Kt — K 2
R — (K 2) — Q 2	27	R — B 5

White has been marking time for the last few moves. His defensive position is at the maximum of its force; it cannot be improved. It is now up to Black to show how to break down the barriers.

Q — R 3	28	K — Kt 2
R — K B 2	29	P — R 4

Black has everything his own way, so he prepares his position until he is ready to force a break.

R — K 2	30	Kt — B 4

Black: J. R. Capablanca

White: A. Nimzovitsch

DIAGRAM 27

White to move. Position after Black's 30th move
Kt — B 4

Black takes the first opportunity to break through. White is forced to take the Kt. Should he play in-

stead R — (K 2) — Q 2 then 31...Kt × Kt; 32
R × Kt (best), R × R; 33 P × R, Q — Kt 4 followed by R — B 8 and Black will win in a similar way
to that of the actual game.

Kt × Kt ch   31   Kt P × Kt

White had played his Q to R 3 hoping to prevent the
recapture with the Kt P. He finds, however, that he
cannot take the R P because of R — K R followed
by R — R 5. The weak K B P of White begins to
tell the story.

Q — B 3   32   K — Kt 3
R — (K 2) — Q 2   33   R — K 5
R — Q 4   34   R — (B) — B 5

Black: J. R. Capablanca

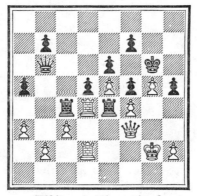

White: A. Nimzovitsch
DIAGRAM 28
White to play. Position after Black's 34th move
R — (B) — B 5

Black forces a second exchange in order to work his
Queen into White's position. The situation in the

diagram is most interesting. Whether White exchanges the Rooks now or later he always loses because of the fact that all the resulting Q endings are lost for White owing to his weak K B P, and to the fact that the Black Queen can work her way in into the open King's position of White.

Q — B 2	35	Q — Kt 4
K — Kt 3	36	R — (B 5) × R
P × R	37	Q — B 5
K — Kt 2	38	P — Kt 4

Again Black is at liberty to do as he pleases; therefore he prepares for all eventualities.

K — Kt	39	P — Kt 5
P × P	40	P × P
K — Kt 2	41	Q — B 8
K — Kt 3	42	Q — K R 8
R — Q 3	43	R — K 8
R — B 3	44	R — Q 8
P — Kt 3	45	R — Q B 8
R — K 3	46	R — K B 8
White resigns	47	

For this game Black was awarded the special prize for the best played game of the Tournament.

8. ENGLISH OPENING P — Q B 4; QUEEN'S GAMBIT
IN EFFECT

(International Masters Tournament, New York, 1927)

White: A. Nimzovitsch   Black: J. R. Capablanca

P — Q B 4	1	Kt — K B 3
Kt — K B 3	2	P — K 3
P — Q 4	3	P — Q 4
P — K 3	4	B — K 2
Q Kt — Q 2	5	

White, during the course of the opening so far, has been changing about the order of the moves. He started with an English opening and after the third move he had already turned it into a Queen's Gambit. Then on his third move he failed to bring out his Q B, and now he makes this move. It may be that he intended to puzzle Black, or that he tried to disguise, until the last minute, what he really intended to play. That can be done by White, up to a certain point, but never at the expense of proper development. White's last move has for object to retake with the Kt in case Black should at any time play Q P × P. It aims also at playing P — K 4 after the K B has been brought out to Q 3.

	5	O — O
B — Q 3	6	P — B 4

To prevent P — K 4 and to take the initiative. This has been possible thanks to the system of opening adopted by White. The fact that Black is able so early in the game to take things into his own hand is sufficient proof that the development of White has been faulty.

$$Q\,P \times P \qquad 7$$

Black: J. R. Capablanca

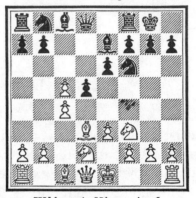

White: A. Nimzovitsch

DIAGRAM 29

Black to play.   Position after White's 7th move
$$Q\,P \times P$$

$$7 \qquad Kt - R\,3$$

The Joker in the position.   Black will retake the P attacking the B with the Kt, gaining Time and Position.   Short of a move gaining material, a move gaining both in Time and Position is an ideal opening move.

White		Black
O — O	8	Kt × P
B — K 2	9	P — Q Kt 3
P × P	10	Kt × P
Kt — Kt 3	11	B — Kt 2
Kt × Kt	12	B × Kt

After his failure in the opening, White, with very good judgement, attempts to simplify the game hoping to overcome the loss of time by bringing about a position where he may through skilful defensive play neutralize Black's advantage in development.

Q — R 4	13	Q — B 3

Black is aware of White's plan. He prepares for one more exchange, at the same time retarding the development of White's Q B.

B — R 6	14	B × B
Q × B	15	Kt — Kt 5
Q — K 2	16	K R — Q

Black keeps on developing his pieces in the most logical way. Outside of the 7th move there is not a single move of Black that is not simple and logical. Any one playing over the game would think that he would have done the same had he been playing the Black pieces. Yet with every move Black is gaining.

P — Q R 3	17	Kt — Q 6
Kt — K	18	Kt × Kt
R × Kt	19	Q R — B
R — Kt	20	

White is at last ready to liberate his position by means of P — Q Kt 4 followed by B — Kt 2. Black, on the other hand, as a result of simple and logical development, has the control of both the open files with his Rooks and is also ahead in Time. It is

Black: J. R. Capablanca

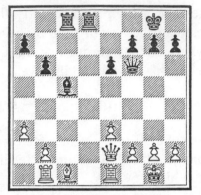

White: A. Nimzovitsch
DIAGRAM 30
Black to play.   Position after White's 20th move
R — Kt

now time to turn his advantage to account before
White is able fully to develop his game.

20   Q — K 4

A finesse to gain time in bringing the Q into the
battle.   Black wants to take possession of the seventh
row with one of his rooks and to do that he needs the
co-operation of the Q.   The text move aims at pre-
venting P — Q Kt 4 at once, which would be answered by 21...B — Q 3; 22 P — Kt 3, Q — K 5
and Black will obtain possession of the seventh row.

P — K Kt 3	21	Q — Q 4
P — Q Kt 4	22	B — B
B — Kt 2	23	Q — R 7
R — R	24	Q — Kt 6
B — Q 4	25	R — B 7

At last Black has possession of the seventh row. Its effect will soon be felt.

| Q — R 6 | 26 | P — K 4 |
| B × K P | 27 | K R — Q 7 |

Black: J. R. Capablanca

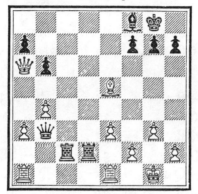

White: A. Nimzovitsch
DIAGRAM 31
White to play. Position after Black's 27th move
K R — Q 7

| Q — Kt 7 | 28 | R × P |

It is now evident that White's game is gone. It should be noticed that White was unable to play 28 R — K B because of 28...Q × K P. (The Queen could not be taken because mate would follow in three moves); and if then 29 B — B 4 29...R × B P, giving up the Q again, and mating in a few moves no matter what White played.

| P — Kt 4 | 29 | Q — K 3 |

Threatening not only Q × P ch but also R × P.

| B — Kt 3 | 30 |

White puts up a fight. If Black were to play
30...Q × Kt P then R — K B would give him a
chance. It is true that with proper play Black would
still be able to win but it would not be as easy as in
the actual game.

30   R × P

The coup de grâce. White cannot take the Rook
because of Q × Kt P ch followed by Q — R 6 and
mate.

Q — B 3	31	R (R 7) — Kt 7 ch
Q × R	32	R × Q ch
K × R	33	Q × Kt P
Q R — Q	34	P — K R 4
R — Q 4	35	Q — Kt 4
K — R 2	36	P — R 4
R — K 2	37	P × P
P × P	38	B — K 2
R — K 4	39	B — B 3
R — K B 2	40	Q — Q 4
R — K 8 ch	41	K — R 2

White resigned.

9. QUEEN'S PAWN OPENING

(International Masters Tournament, Berlin, 1928)

White: J. R. Capablanca   Black: A. Rubinstein

P — Q 4	1	P — Q 4
Kt — K B 3	2	P — Q B 4

This is an attempt to take the initiative away from
White. What is best now is difficult to say, but on

general theory Black's move should be faulty, because the second player cannot, without serious risk,
pretend to take the initiative so early in the game
against a natural developing move like Kt — K B 3.

| P × P | 3 | P — K 3 |
| P — K 4 | 4 | |

White plays to leave Black with an isolated centre
Pawn. The drawback to this system is that it permits Black to develop his pieces without the slightest
trouble. The isolated centre Pawn, however, is a
weakness which keeps Black occupied all the time.
It is yet to be proved, however, whether or not that
weakness is enough to justify the form of development adopted by White in this game.

| | 4 | B × P |

Of course not P × P because of 5 Q × Q, K × Q;
6 Kt — Kt 5.

| P × P | 5 | P × P |
| B — Kt 5 ch | 6 | |

White plays to castle quickly, before devoting his attention to the isolated Pawn. The drawback to this
move is that sooner or later the B will have to come
back either to Q 3 or K 2, thus losing time.

	6	Kt — Q B 3
O — O	7	Kt — K 2
Q Kt — Q 2	8	

An essential manœuvre in this type of position. The
Kt will go Kt 3 and later P — Q B 3 will be played

so as to fix the P at Q 4. Otherwise the P would be free to advance without risk.

	8	O — O
Kt — Kt 3	9	B — Kt 3
R -- K	10	

To take the open file and to prepare for the eventual B — K 3, getting rid of the powerful B at Kt 3. Some annotators have claimed that this was a weak move for White. That is not so. The text move is an excellent move which could hardly be improved upon in this position.

10   B — Kt 5

Black: A. Rubinstein

White: J. R. Capablanca

DIAGRAM 32

White to play. Position after Black's 10th move
B — Kt 5

This is a vital point in the game. Black is now fully developed and threatens to play B × P ch followed by Q — Kt 3. White could play B — K 3, but then

P — Q 5 would upset the cart. White, however, could and should have played 11 P — K R 3. If then B × Kt, 12 Q × B would give White an excellent game and if 11...B — R 4; 12 P — B 3 would again give White the best of it, since the Black Kt at K 2 could not go to either Kt 3 or B 4 because of P — Kt 4. White made a mistake by playing 11 B — Q 3.

B — Q 3	11	Kt — Kt 3
P — K R 3	12	B × Kt
Q × B	13	Q Kt — K 4
Q — B 5	14	Kt × B
Q × Kt	15	

Black: A. Rubinstein

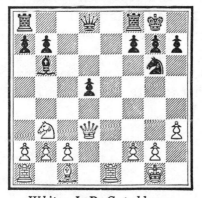

White: J. R. Capablanca
DIAGRAM 33
Black to play.   Position after White's 15th move
Q × Kt

This is the turning point of the game. As a result of White's weak eleventh move Black has obtained a very good game. His only weak point is the isolated Q P and he could now get rid of it by playing 15 Q —

B 3, as White would have nothing better than B —
K 3. This would have led to a practically even game.
Thus 15...Q — B 3; 16 B — K 3, Q × Kt P;
17 Q × P, B × B; 18 R × B. It may be that Black
thought he should do better than draw and was in
consequence lured into making the text move.

15   P — Q 5

From the point of view of the safety of the Pawn,
this is a natural enough move, but it is strategically
wrong unless there is more than an even chance of
advancing it still farther. In its present position the
Pawn blocks the line of action of the strongly posted
B at Kt 3. The Pawn itself is now protected by the
B as well as the Q, but on the other hand it is also
attacked twice. There is one advantage in having it
at Q 5, namely that the White Q B P cannot advance.
But again that is an advantage provided that Black
is able either to defend the P at Q 5 or to attack the
Q B P of White.

B — Q 2   16   Q — B 3
R — K 4   17   Q R — Q

This may not be the best. Possibly the other Rook
should have gone there in order to have one Rook at
Q square and the other at Q B square attacking the
Q B P. Black, however, is already contemplating an
exchange of Rooks and for that purpose the text
move is necessary.

Q R — K   18   Q — B 3
P — Kt 3   19

A very important move. It completely blocks the action of the Kt at K Kt 3, and makes room for the King at K Kt 2. The fact that there is no B along the white diagonals makes the K position safe enough, since White controls the only open file with his Rooks.

		19	K R — K
B — R 5		20	R × R
Q × R		21	

Black: A. Rubinstein

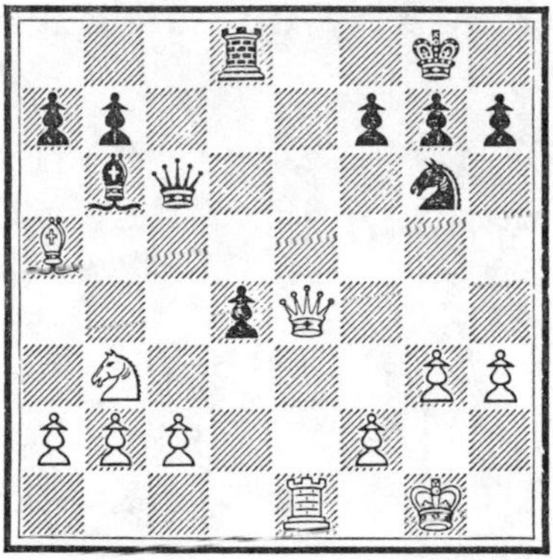

White: J. R. Capablanca

DIAGRAM 34

Black to move. Position after White's 21st move
Q × R

The position is very interesting and will repay study. From now on White is able to force the game. At present White threatens B × B, Q × B, R — Q winning the Q P. Black's best chance would be Q × Q, R × Q, B × B, Kt × B, P — B 4.

	21	Kt — B

Black plays to bring the Kt to K 3 to the defence of his Pawn. This gives White the chance, however, to get to the seventh rank with his Rook, and as a result Black will soon have to lose a Pawn. At this stage of the game, however, it was extremely difficult to decide on the course to take.

Q × Q	22	P × Q
R — K 7	23	R — Q 4

White threatened to play R × R P. The alternative was 23...P — Q 6; 24 P × P, R × P; 25 B × B, P × B; 26 R — Kt 7 with a slight advantage for White.

B × B	24	P × B
R — Kt 7	25	Kt — Q 2
R — B 7	26	R — Q 3

If 26...P — Q B 4; 27 R — B 8 ch, Kt — B; 28 R — Kt 8, P — B 5; 29 Kt — Q 2, P — Q 6; 30 P × P

R — B 8 ch	27	Kt — B
Kt — Q 2	28	P — Q B 4

If 28...P — Q Kt 4, 29 Kt — Kt 3 followed by Kt — R 5.

Kt — B 4	29	R — K 3
R — Kt 8	30	R — K 8 ch
K — Kt 2	31	P — K Kt 4
P — Q R 4	32	R — Q R 8
Kt × P	33	K — Kt 2

The King is free at last, but too late. The constant mating threats which forced Black to keep his Kt to guard his King made it possible for White to win a Pawn and with it the game.

R — B 8	34	Kt — K 3
Kt — Q 7	35	R × P
Kt × P	36	R — Kt 5

Black cannot afford to exchange Knights because the
Q P would be lost.

Kt — Q 3	37	R — Kt 4
K — B 3	38	P — R 3
P — Q Kt 4	39	P — R 4
P — Kt 4	40	P × P ch
P × P	41	P — B 3
R — B 4	42	K — B 2
Kt — B 5	43	Kt — Q
Kt — Kt 3	44	Resigns

A very hard struggle.

10. QUEEN'S GAMBIT IN FACT

(Euwe-Capablanca Match, Holland, 1930)
Third Game of the Match

White: J. R. Capablanca   Black: Dr. M. Euwe

P — Q 4	1	Kt — K B 3
P — Q B 4	2	P — K 3
Kt — Q B 3	3	B — Kt 5
Q — B 2	4	P — Q 4
P × P	5	P × P
B — Kt 5	6	Q — Q 3

To unpin the Kt. To go back with the B would
bring about a regular variation of the Q's Gambit
with Black a move behind. To play P — K R 3 and
P — K Kt 4 would be too risky.

P — K 3	7	Kt — K 5	
B — K B 4	8	Q — K Kt 3	

The alternatives would be Q — K 2 or Q — Q B 3. The other Queen moves are much less satisfactory. It should be noticed that in the eight moves played so far, Black has moved his Queen twice and his K Kt twice also. In a close position such things are often possible and good, but in a rather open position they can very seldom be done without getting into trouble.

P — Q R 3	9

Black threatened Kt × Kt. The text move forces Black to exchange the B for the Kt, thereby not only releasing the pressure against the Q Kt and the K, but also strengthening White's position.

	9	B × Kt ch	
P × B	10	B — B 4	

This involves the loss of a Pawn, but Black had very little choice. The only way to avoid immediate loss would be to play Q — Q B 3, another Queen move in ten. 10...P — Q B 3 was not feasible because of 11 P — B 3, Kt — B 3; 12 B — Q 3, Q — R 4; 13 P — K R 4 and Black cannot stop P — Kt 4 winning a piece.

White		Black
Q — Kt 3	11	O — O

Black plays for the attack. He is slightly ahead in development and now offers a Pawn in order to gain more time. Should White play Q × Kt P, Kt —

Black: Dr. Max Euwe

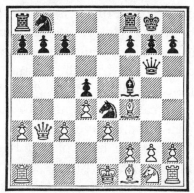

White: J. R. Capablanca
DIAGRAM 35
White to play.   Position after Black's 11th move
O — O

Q B 3 would give Black such an advantage in development that it would be impossible for White to avoid serious loss.   White, however, could have played Q × Q P and obtained the better game thus: 12 Q × Q P, Kt × Q B P; 13 Q — Kt 3, Kt — K 5; 14 Kt — B 3, Q — Kt 3 (best; if 14...Kt — B 3, 15 R — B, Kt — Q 3; 16 Kt — K 5, Kt × Kt; 17 P × Kt with a winning position); 15 Q × Q, B P × Q; 16 B — Q 3 with what should be a winning position.   White could also play 12 Kt — B 3 and obtain a winning game since Black's best answer would be Q — Kt 3 and then would follow Q × Q, B P × Q; P — B 4. Instead of adopting the simple course White went in for complications: a policy not to be advised when there is a simple continuation in sight offering a definite advantage.

P — B 3	12	Kt — Q 3
P — Kt 4	13	B — Q 6

Black insists in playing an attack at all costs: a wrong policy in a case like this where the number of pieces for the attack is inferior to the number of pieces for the defence. Black could succeed only if he were able to throw into the fray the balance of his pieces before White could bring his to the defence. Since that is not the case he is bound to suffer the consequences. He should have played B — K 3, when White would probably have played R — Q in order to start an attack against Black's King through B — Q 3. The continuation 13...B — K 3; 14 B × Kt, P × B; 15 Q × Kt P, Kt — Q 2 would give White a very doubtful game.

Q × Q P	14	B × B
K × B	15	Q — Q 6 ch
Kt — K 2	16	Kt — B 5
K — B 2	17	Kt × K P

Black: Dr. Max Euwe

White: J. R. Capablanca

DIAGRAM 36

White to play. Position after Black's 17th move
Kt × K P

A very clever sacrifice. White cannot take the Kt
because of R — K which would regain the piece for
Black with a good game. But unfortunately for
Black he has not enough force for the attack. All he
is attacking with is a Queen and a Knight, and the
only other piece he can throw immediately into the
battle is the K R. Against that White has all his
pieces ready to go to the defence of his King. Under
such conditions, unless the position is of a very unusual nature, the attack cannot succeed.

Q × P	18	Kt — R 3
Q — Kt	19	Q × Q

Black had to exchange Queens to avoid the loss of the
Kt. As a result White comes out a Pawn ahead with
a good game, advantage enough to win with proper
play.

Q R × Q	20	Kt — B 5
P — Q R 4	21	Q R — Kt
R — Kt 5	22	R — Kt 3
K R — Q Kt	23	R — K
Kt — Kt 3	24	R — K B 3
R — K B 5	25	

White wants to keep his B at B 4 where it controls
the moves of the two Black Kts. At the same time
he wants to place his Kt at K 4 in order to block any
possible entrance of the Rook at K sq into White's
position. The Kt at K 4 would be in a very strong
central position. It is true that as a result of this
manœuvre Black will be able to reunite his Q's side
Pawns and also White's pieces will be crowding one

another a little, but as White's ultimate intention is to advance on the K's side, the overcrowding of White's pieces will not become too serious a fault. The alternatives would be either Kt — B 5 or B — B threatening Kt — K 4. The first move would prevent the placing of the Kt at K 4. The second move would remove the B from the one square where he controls most of the moves of both the Black Knights. The course of the game vindicated White's judgement in playing the text move.

	25	R — Q Kt 3
R × R	26	R P × R
Kt — K 4	27	P — K B 3
P — R 4	28	P — B 3
P — K R 5	29	K — B 2

Black could not play 29...P — R 3 because of 30 B × P.

B — B	30

A bad move. White should have gone on with his original plan, which would have won without much trouble thus: 30 P — R 6, R × Kt; 31 P × R, P — Kt 3; 32 R — Q Kt 5, P × R; 33 P × P and White would regain the piece with a won position. White made the text move forgetting that it released the Kt at Q R 3. Incidentally it has been assumed by all annotators that Black could now easily draw by playing 30...Kt — B 2. They have stated that against 30...Kt — B 2, White could not play 31 P — R 5 because of Kt — Q 4, threatening to win the R by P — Kt 3. The assertion is entirely wrong. Not

only can White play P — R 5 but it is the best move,
and the one move that gives White the best winning
chances.   The position is so interesting that it will
repay study.

Black: Dr. Max Euwe

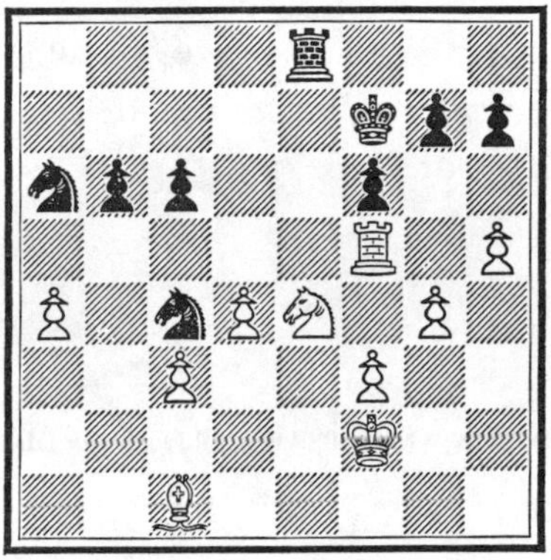

White: J. R. Capablanca
DIAGRAM 37
Black to play.   Position after White's 30th move
B — B

Suppose that Black played 30...Kt — B 2; 31 P —
R 5, Kt — Q 4; 32 P × P, P — Kt 3; 33 R — B 4,
R — Q Kt; 34 Kt × P, Kt × R; 35 B × Kt, R ×
P; 36 Kt × P and with three Pawns for the exchange
White has an excellent chance to win.   Let us go back
again.   30...Kt — B 2; 31 P — R 5, Kt — Q 4;
32 P × P, P — Kt 3; 34 R — B 4, R — K 2;
35 Kt — Kt 5 ch followed by R — K 4 with winning
chances.   From the above it follows that after 30...
Kt — B 2; 31 P — R 5, Kt — Q 4; 32 P × P, P —
Kt 3; 33 R — B 4 Black's best chance for a draw is
to play 33...Kt × R; 34 B × Kt, Kt × P; 35 Kt —
Q 6 ch, K — K 2; 36 Kt × R, K × Kt; 37 K — K 2

and while it would be hard to prove a win, White would have chances for victory.

Actually the game continued:

30   R — K 3

A blunder due to time pressure. The game was being played at the rate of 32 moves in two hours. Black was very short of time and probably tired from the ordeal.

Kt — Kt 5 ch   31   Resigns.

11. QUEEN'S GAMBIT DECLINED. SLAV DEFENCE

White: J. R. Capablanca   Black: Dr. M. Euwe

P — Q 4	1	P — Q 4
Kt — K B 3	2	Kt — K B 3
P — Q B 4	3	P — B 3
Kt — B 3	4	P × P
P — Q R 4	5	B — B 4
Kt — K 5	6	Q Kt — Q 2
Kt × Q B P	7	Q — B 2
P — K Kt 3	8	P — K 4
P × P	9	Kt × P
B — B 4	10	K Kt — Q 2
B — Kt 2	11	B — K 3

P — K B 3 is the natural move. The text move is artificial and loses time; therefore it should be inferior to P — K B 3.

Kt × Kt	12	Kt × Kt
O — O	13	Q — R 4

As a result of his 11th move Black is practically compelled to make a second move with his Queen before full development has taken place.   In a position as open as the one in this game such loss of time should be avoided.

Kt — K 4	14	R — Q
Q — B 2	15	B — K 2

B — Q Kt 5 was the alternative, but Black wants to guard against Kt — Kt 5.

Black: Dr. Max Euwe

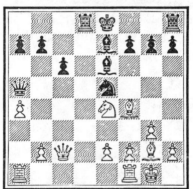

White: J. R. Capablanca
DIAGRAM 38
White to play.   Position after Black's 15th move
B — K 2

The position is very interesting.   White could play 16 Kt — Kt 5, B × Kt; 17 B × B, P — B 3 (not Kt — B 6 ch, because of 18 P × Kt, Q × B; 19 P — B 4, Q — Q R 4; 20 P — Q Kt 4 with advantage for White); 18 B — B 4 and White would have two Bishops and a good game.   There was, however, a chance to make a combination which might give White a decisive advantage. Hence White's next move, which was a surprise to Black.

P — Q Kt 4   16   B × P

He could of course refuse the Pawn and play Q — B 2, but that would not help his position at all and would be a condemnation of his 13th move Q — R 4. In fact it looks as though Q — B 2 could not be played without losing a Pawn. Thus 16...Q — B 2; 17 Kt — B 5, B — B; 18 Q — K 4, P — B 3; 19 Kt — Q 3, B — Q 3; 20 P — Kt 5, P — Q B 4; 21 Q R — B, P — Q Kt 3; 22 B × Kt, P × B; 23 P — B 4 and White wins a Pawn with a very strong position besides.

Q — Kt 2   17   P — B 3
K R — Kt   18

Black: Dr. Max Euwe

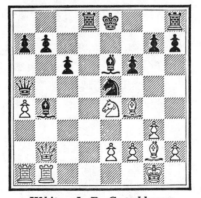

White: J. R. Capablanca
DIAGRAM 39
Black to move. Position after White's 18th move
K R — Kt

This is a mistake leading to all kinds of complications. By simply playing the other Rook to Kt, White would have won at least a Pawn with a very safe position. Thus: 18 Q R — Kt, B — K 2 (best); 19 Q × Kt P, K — B 2 (best); 20 B × Kt, Q × B; 21 Q × B P and White has a Pawn more and a safe game. Naturally, in all these positions under consideration, White cannot at any time play Q × B, because of R — Q 8 ch. For instance, if Black plays 18...Kt — B 5, White cannot play 19 Q × B, because of 19...R — Q 8 ch. 20 B — B, Q × Q. 21 R × Q, R × R leaving Black with a Rook for a B and a good position besides, enough to win the game. The text move, however, is extremely difficult to answer. The experts watching the game thought that Kt — B 5 would win for Black. The position is worth considering.

Now suppose that Black played Kt — B 5, then: 19 Kt × P ch, K — B 2 (best); 20 Q × B, R — Q 8 ch; 21 R × R, Q × Q; 22 Kt — K 4 and White would have a R and Kt for the Q and a terrific attack which most probably could not be stopped. For instance: 22...R — K (probably best); 23 Q R — Kt, Q — R 4 (probably best. If Q × P, Kt — B 5); 24 Kt — Kt 5 ch, K — Kt 3 (if K — Kt, Kt × B, R × Kt, R × P); 25 R — Q 4 and Black probably will be unable to protect White's many threats. Really a most remarkable position.

	18	O — O
B × Kt	19	P × B
Kt — Kt 5	20	

Black: Dr. Max Euwe

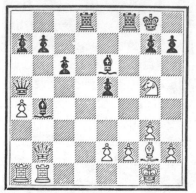

White: J. R. Capablanca

DIAGRAM 40

Black to move. Position after White's 20th move
Kt — Kt 5

Of course if 20 Q × B, R — Q 8 ch; 21 B — B, Q × Q and wins.

20   B — B 6

Not the best. Black's defence is extremely difficult. It is touch and go, yet 20...B — B 2 would probably save the game. After the text move White wins by force.

White		Black
Q — B 2	21	B — B 4
B — K 4	22	P — K Kt 3

Of course if B × R; 23 B × B and Black must lose his other Bishop because of the threat B — K 6 ch followed by Q × P mate. Black, however, might have tried 22...P — K R 3; 23 B × B, P × Kt;

24 R — R 3 and White would have an easy win on account of the exposed position of the Black K.

Q — R 2 ch	23	K — Kt 2
R × P ch	24	R — Q 2
Q R — Kt	25	Q — R 3
Q — Kt 3	26	R × R
Q × R ch	27	Q × Q
R × Q ch	28	K — Kt
B × P	29	R — Q
R × Q R P	30	R — Q 3
B — K 4	31	B — Q 2
P — K R 4	32	B — Q 5
R — R 8 ch	33	K — Kt 2
P — K 3	34	B — B 6
B — B 3	35	Resigns